BE MY GUEST

This book is dedicated to Nan, who always believed I could do it, to Mum, who would be proud to know that I could do it, and to my agent Jennifer Kavanagh, who stood behind me with a knotted bullwhip and *made* me do it.

ANNE SUTER

BE MY GUEST

FOREWORD BY

HANNAH GORDON

Illustrations by Patrick Wright

W H ALLEN

Printed and bound in Great Britain by
Mackays of Chatham PLC, Chatham, Kent
for the publishers
W H Allen & Co Plc, Sekforde House
135–179 St John Street, London EC1V 4LL

ISBN 0-491-03604-3

Grateful acknowledgement is given for the kind permission to quote from the following: *Backstairs Life in a Country House* by Eileen Balderson and Douglas Goodland, David and Charles; *Heartbreak House* by George Bernard Shaw, The Society of Authors on behalf of the Bernard Shaw Estate; *Afterthoughts* by Logan Pearsall Smith, Constable; *Service with a Smile* by P G Wodehouse, Century Hutchinson Ltd, *The Pursuit of Love* by Nancy Mitford, Peters Fraser and Dunlop Group Ltd; *Etiquette for Every Occasion* by Angela Lansbury, B T Batsford; *Evelyn Waugh's Letters* ed. M Amory, Weidenfeld and Nicolson; *The Future of Mankind* by Bertrand Russell, Unwin Hyman; *The Young Visitors*, Daisy Ashford; 'There's a Small Hotel' © 1936 Chappell & Co Inc, 'Mrs Otis Regrets' © 1934 Harms Inc, 'And Thank You So Much Mrs Lowsborough-Goodby' © 1934 Harms Inc, all reproduced by permission of Warner Chappell Music Ltd.

CONTENTS

FOREWORD

The evening I sank, exhausted, in a heap to read Anne Suter's entertaining and very funny book *Be My Guest*, I had just waved goodbye to the last of a stream of visitors, and I can only assume that she must have been a fly on the wall.

How did she know that beneath my calm, well-organized, fun-loving exterior, there lurked a desperate woman; who, if she had to produce just one more well-balanced, effortless meal would flip her lid and whose only ambitions left in life were to eat boiled eggs and soldiers and be in bed by 10.30pm.

They say the basic requirement for good comedy is that it should be firmly rooted in reality. Anyone who reads Miss Suter's book will recognize themselves as I certainly did and more than once. She had me laughing out loud and smiling a good deal as she leads us through the machinations we all get up to when entertaining visitors.

Conversely, as she steers us through the catalogue of familiar disasters that can befall us in other peoples' houses, one realizes how right she is to extoll the virtues of a good hotel.

Miss Suter with a delicious sense of fun has a go at us all including presumably her own friends, but she does it in such a disarming and witty way, that no one could take offence. In fact there are lessons to be learned by any would-be hostess or guest.

A book that's good for dipping into when you need a laugh – an ideal present; and a *must* for any guest room.

Hannah Gordon

'THE PLEASURE OF YOUR COMPANY IS REQUESTED . . . '

WILL YOU WON'T YOU . . . ?

Lewis Carroll, *Alice's Adventures in Wonderland*

For those seeking guidance on the correct wording of an invitation or its reply, one need look no further than the example provided by a young lady with a sharp eye for social behaviour.

My Dear Alfred,
I want you to come for a stop with me so I have sent you a top hat wrapped up in tishu paper inside the box. Will you wear it staying with me because it is very uncommon. Please bring one of your young ladies whichever is the prettiest in the face.

I remain,
Yours truely,

BERNARD CLARK

To which, after he had sat down and eaten the egg which Ethel had so kindly laid for him, Alfred replied:

My Dear Bernard,
Certainly I shall come and stay with you next Monday I will bring Ethel Monticue commonly called Miss M. She is very active and pretty. I do hope I shall enjoy myself with you. I am fond of digging in the garden and I am parshial to ladies if they are nice I suppose it is my nature. I am not quite a

gentleman but you would hardly notice it but cant be helped anyhow. We shall come by the 3-15.

Your old and valud friend

ALFRED SALTEENA"

Thus Bernard Clark and Mr. Salteena in Daisy Ashford's *The Young Visiters*.

In modern times it is, perhaps, unnecessary to accompany the invitation with the present of a top hat, but that apart, this example could hardly be improved upon.

BE MY GUEST

> To see her standing at the top of an expensively horticultural staircase receiving her husband's guests was rather like watching an animal performing on a music-hall stage. One always tells oneself that the animal likes it and one always knows it doesn't.
>
> 'Saki', *The Unbearable Bassington*

No don't. Oh please don't! Please don't be my guest. You probably wouldn't enjoy the experience, and I most certainly would not. As the hostess with the leastest I am thinking of having a specially hand-woven 'Unwelcome' mat to put in front of my door.

I wish I had lived when an Englishman's home really WAS his castle. I could have kept the drawbridge permanently in the 'up' position, and had vats of boiling oil always ready on the ramparts to pour down on prospective guests. In a des. res. in suburbia one has no such defences. One just receives unexpected telephone calls from cousins in Cumberland who say that on their way to London they have some business to do in one's area, so can they come and stay for a couple of nights? One longs to ask if they have never heard of that excellent institution known as the hotel, but politeness demands that one bites back this instinctive reaction and instead murmurs through clenched teeth the stereotyped lie about loving to have them.

I think Alexander Graham Bell has a lot to answer for. Before he invented the telephone you would get these requests in writing, which allowed a lot more thinking time in which to concoct a plausible excuse, or, as a last resort, to reply in a manner calculated to make Cumberland cousins feel that one was not exactly prepared to go out and kill the fatted calf for them.

'Of course we'll be delighted to have you. I'm afraid Priscilla will still be in quarantine, but it probably won't be catching by then.' (Never name the disease. They will say they have had it.)

'Of course we'll be delighted to have you. We've just started re-papering the house from top to bottom and another pair of hands will be a god-send.'

'Of course we'll be delighted to have you. We're being hosts to the Tower Hamlets Unmarried Mothers and Children Annual Outing on Sunday, and you will be a marvellous help.'

Cumberland cousins have to be asking for trouble if they pursue the matter after any of these responses.

If driven to extremes, there is always:

> Dear Niece,
> So you are after your rights at last. Well, I have expected to hear from Robert Poste's child these last twenty years.
>
> Child, my man once did your father a great wrong. If you will come to us I will do my best to atone, but you must never ask what for. My lips are sealed.
>
> We are not like other folk, maybe, but there have always been Starkadders at Cold Comfort, and we will do our best to welcome Robert Poste's child.
>
> Child, child, if you come to this doomed house, what is to save you? Perhaps you may be able to help us when our hour comes.
>
> Yr. Affec. Aunt,
> J. Starkadder.
>
> (Flora Poste's letter in *Cold Comfort Farm* by Stella Gibbons.)

I must try to keep that phrase, 'So you are after your rights at last,' on the tip of my tongue in anticipation of the next long-distance call from Cumberland.

Actually, cousins rate among the less troublesome of unwanted visitors. Being 'Family' they can be meted out the kind of rough justice deserved by self-invited guests.

It is when you come actually to inviting people – people to

whom you owe hospitality, people for whom you will have to make an effort, people who (if the truth were told) would probably much rather stay snugly in their own homes—that your troubles really begin.

'We really must ask the Beavers to say.'

'Why?'

'Well, we owe them.'

'Why?'

'Oh, don't be silly. You remember we went to stay with them the weekend of their garden party, about two and a half years ago.'

'Oh, God yes, I remember THAT. Well for Heaven's sake don't ask them for too long.'

'They had us for an extended weekend.'

'Must it be a weekend? Can't you ask them during the week, when I'm not here?'

'Don't be silly.'

So a cloying letter is sent to the Beavers, oozing anxiety for the pleasure of their company with every comma, and you sit back and hope that by some miracle they cannot come.

It is unwise to put your faith in miracles. The Beavers will be THRILLED to accept and are, apparently, aquiver with anticipation of the moment when they can come and throw a monumental spanner in the works of your well-ordered routine. Of course they will have an aunt from Johannesburg staying with them at that time and hope it won't be too much for you if they bring her too. They know how much she'd enjoy meeting you. Luckily they do not know how little the feeling is reciprocated.

So the die is cast and you are committed to feeding and watering, entertaining, and generally slaving round the house after the Beavers and their South African appendage.

Hope springing, as it does, eternal in the human breast, you will have fixed the date of the visit as far in the future as possible with the vague feeling that events fixed at a distant date do not actually take place. They do. Beaver, Beaver & Co., will be standing on your doorstep before you have even had time to sweep it. Before you have had time to sweep the rest of the house either. Preparations for the reception of guests are long, arduous and fraught with the complications of trying to find all the things that you put away 'in a safe place' after the departure of your last guests, and for which you now have a pressing need again.

It will only be long after the departure of the Beavers that all the things you were searching for will turn up. In the meantime, in one of the brief interludes between the scrubbing, washing, cooking, painting, mending and ironing which are all part of the rich pattern of preparations for receiving guests, you will have dashed out and bought replacements. In theory, therefore, you should then be equipped with duplicates of all the essentials for entertaining, but the theory never works out. Long before the next onslaught of visitors, you will have mislaid the lot.

PREPARING TO BE A DUTIFUL HOSTESS

Any experienced hostess knows that if guests who have come to stay are going to enjoy themselves and feel at ease in her house the 'take us as you find us' cult is not really a workable arrangement.

Betty Messenger, *The Complete Guide to Etiquette*

Actually it doesn't really matter if the Beavers, or their equivalents, come trailing clouds of relatives or not. Just one single guest causes as much havoc in a household as two, three, or any number more, and requires the same amount of preparation.

As the day of doom approaches the hostess will suddenly realise that the spare bed is not made up because the last visitor had put his foot through the rather thin bottom sheet (a relic from someone's schooldays) and she has forgotten to replace it. This will require a hasty dive into that drawer underneath the bed where all those lovely sheets, left to her by old Granny Wetherby and kept in protective plastic for just such an occasion, are readily to hand. Only they are not. The hostess has forgotten that over the years she has given them away to sundry sons and daughters moving out of home, or offered them as covering for the trestle tables at the Vicarage tea party, and the Vicar's wife has never returned them. If by any freak of fate they actually *are* still there in their plastic covering, they will turn out to be riddled with moth holes, and/or will have deep brown stains imprinted down every fold and crease. The hostess will be obliged to rush out and spend hours comparing the relative prices of cheap sheets at Marks and Spencers and British Home Stores and finally purchase a pair which will get lost in the wash on the following laundry day. The whole process will then be ready to start all over again.

Admittedly if there is more than one guest it entails buying more sheets, but the basic situation is always the same. It is only the quantity which varies.

One area in which the number of guests actually does make a difference is the pillow section. Hands up all readers who have sufficient pillows to cope with the sudden invasion of guests in quantity? No, I thought not. Pillow cases you may have. They will be in Granny Wetherby's drawer with those brown folds down the middle, but the pillows themselves are not things that you can pop away and forget. Pillows are voluminous and need space, so most households have only the minimum requirement and are thrown into a tizzy of robbing Peter to pay Paul whenever the prospect of multiple guests looms on the horizon – Paul in this case representing the guests and Peter one's own household in ascending order of vulnerability. Children, if there are any, get thrown to the wall first, and if not, one ends up pillowless oneself, or sharing one between two. The only thing to be said in favour of this practice is that it is a very good mender of creaking marriages. It is difficult to sustain a state of boiling fury with someone whose nose is only two centimetres away from one's own, which proves, I suppose, that guests can, occasionally, have their uses.

Nowadays timid guests may be press-ganged into bringing their own sheets, or even sleeping bags, with them (a process which takes on an entirely different aspect when you yourself are the invitee instead of the inviter), but it would be a brave hostess who would attempt to bludgeon anyone into staggering across country clutching a couple of pillows in addition to their routine luggage. I can think of nowhere where I might be asked to stay which would be worth such an effort, unless perhaps it were Buckingham Palace, but one hardly thinks Her Majesty would make such demands on a loyal subject.

A quick survey of the bedroom just before the invasion reveals all the things that you had been meaning to have 'seen to' ever since you last had someone to stay, and have never quite got round to. Because you never have the necessity of pulling them you have forgotten that the curtains not only do not quite meet in the middle, (having been transferred from the bathroom in your old house and just put up temporarily 'for the time being' when you moved in ten years ago) but that one of them keeps falling off the end because some over-enthusiastic guest once yanked too hard and displaced the screw which is supposed to anchor it in place. You make your routine feeble search for said screw (which has obviously been gobbled up by the Hoover long since) and then, as always, stuff up the end of the rail with a piece of plasticine and hope that it will hold. (It never does.)

You have forgotten too that you have never put into practice the vow that you made to yourself to get the catch on the window fixed directly after the departure of your last guest – six months ago. The wind is still whistling with a scream that would do credit to any Banshee, and no amount of hammering at it with the heel of your shoe will budge the catch one iota, any more than it did the last time. You just have to hope that your guest is a fresh air fiend with a preference for draughts.

A swift survey of the wardrobe reveals a total lack of hangers. (Was your last guest a kleptomaniac or have the rest of the family been scrounging again?) The robbing Peter to pay Paul process starts afresh and leaves a lot of the household's garments hanging on the floor.

Somehow, since it was last inhabited, the spare room has become a dumping ground for all those things that you cannot find a place for elsewhere in the house. There is that broken vase which you have been meaning to mend, a quantity of skiing gear which only comes into use once a year, a black plastic sack full of jumble which you forgot to put out for the Boy Scouts, and a whole lot of presents which you received last Christmas, did not like, and intend giving to someone else next Christmas. (Remember to check to see if one is from your prospective guests, and so needs to be dug out and prominently displayed.)

All this reposes in the middle of the bed.

You gather everything up in your arms and then find that the root problem still applies – you cannot find a place for it anywhere else in the house. The skiing gear can be dumped unceremoniously into the bedrooms of its respective owners, but for the rest it either means struggling with the loft ladder (which is kept at the far end of the garage and so entails a great deal of preliminary manoeuvring of cars) or a quick dash to the local Charity Shop, which will be shut, because it only opens on even dates, and this is an odd one. You will return to it the following day and then spend the rest of your life regretting the loss of half the things you gave away.

The bathroom will also require attention, and you will gaze around it with new eyes, wondering why on earth you have never got round to having that awful brown stain under the hot tap removed long ago, as you have always been meaning to, and noting that the shower still hangs at a drunken angle due to one screw having long since fallen out and disappeared, and realizing that nothing can be done about it without rawl plugs, of which there are none in the house.

Inevitably all those little fancy towels with hand-embroidered daisies on them have disappeared from the linen cupboard (probably in the suitcase of some departing guest, you think savagely) and all those that are left look as though they were usually used for drying the family dog. You hastily grab the ones from your own room, and wash them through in preparation for your guests, wondering the while what they've done to deserve them, appropriate the dog towels for your own use, making a vow to go out and buy a whole lot of new ones the moment after the guest has gone. This is a vow you will not keep.

It always seems to me ironic that people who lead perfectly normal, scruffy lives in their own homes, suddenly need to be treated like royalty when they descend on other people's. It is not 'done', for instance to leave a half used piece of soap on the guest's hand basin (though the betting is they have left a half used piece of soap on their basin back home). Oh no, for a guest you always have to unwrap a new piece, and not just any old piece, either. It has to be smelling of carnations and matching the wallpaper. You are expected too, to go out and

buy an armful of glossy magazines, (costing roughly the price of the Kohinoor), for their bedside table, none of which they will even glance at, far preferring to pinch *Moll Flanders* from your bookshelf, and fail to return it. You are expected to ask them if they like tea or coffee for breakfast, instead of taking what the rest of the family has and lumping it, which is invariably what you have to do when you go away yourself.

It is little wonder that, after all the toil and hassle of the preparations the poor hostess is so worn out that when the moment comes for her to fling wide the front door and greet the guest with a dazzling smile and the words, 'Oh there you are! How lovely to see you!' all her natural instincts are towards drawing the curtains, bolting the doors, battening down the hatches and shouting 'Not at home!' through the letter-box.

A QUESTION OF TASTE

> *November 10th* – Last two days very, very trying, owing to unexpected discovery that Cissie Crabbe is strictly on a diet. This causes Robert to take a dislike to her. Utter impossibility of obtaining lentils OR lemons at short notice makes housekeeping unduly difficult. Mademoiselle in the middle of lunch insists on discussing diet question, and several times exclaimed *Ah, mon doux St. Joseph!* which I consider profane, and beg her never to repeat.
>
> E. M. Delafield, *The Diary of a Provincial Lady*

Once their living accommodation has been made (roughly) habitable, attention must be turned to feeding the brutes.

You will then decide to be a really organised hostess and sit down and plan and write out menus for the whole of your guests' stay, and at the end of this exercise other members of the family will read it through and say helpful things like, 'Ugh!', or 'Oh God, I hate that', or 'Why are we being so posh? We never have things like this normally'.

The one thing that it is wise to verify beforehand is that your guest has not suddenly embraced some cranky diet, so that, after you have been slaving away for hours over a hot stove, preparing a delicious repast with meticulous care, he or she will not suddenly say:

a) 'Oh, by the way, I forgot to tell you, I've become a Vegan.'
b) 'I should have told you not to bother getting anything for me. I've brought my own goatsmilk yogurt and dried figs.'

c) 'I'm afraid because of my condition I have to have everything passed through a hair sieve.'

d) 'I'm so sorry, but the doctor has said I must completely cut out chicken/steak/salmon', or whatever particular delicacy you have been patiently preparing for the past two and a half hours.

Diets apart, no hostess, if she values her sanity, should ever enquire her guests' feeding preferences in advance. The kind of things visitors usually demand (with an agonizingly twee, 'I wonder if it would be too much trouble for you to get . . . ?') tend to be things which can only be bought in two pound packets or two litre jars, and as they are things which would never normally darken the hostess's kitchen cupboard they will clutter up her shelves until the moment that they finally moulded into decay and she chucks them out. This moment will occur one week before the same guest arrives for another visit and with grinding teeth she will be forced to re-stock.

Guests should never be asked if they like Indian or China tea. They will always choose whichever the hostess hasn't got and doesn't like.

Neither should guests who bleat about their need for decaffeinated coffee be pandered to in any way if the hostess doesn't normally keep it in the house. The easiest way to deal with this situation is just to nod, smile sweetly, go into the kitchen, pour out the required number of cups of normal coffee, return with one slightly apart on the tray and thrust it towards the guest saying, 'That's yours'. The guest may or may not then spend a sleepless night, but will have no grounds (unintended pun) for complaint against the coffee.

Guests must be made to realize that enough is enough and the moment when the hostess slumps stuffingless in an armchair, after a decathlon of cooking and washing-up, is not the time to start demanding extras. My sister-in-law vividly recalls the first time a son brought a girl friend home for the weekend. At the son's insistence the boat was right royally pushed out, and the first evening, after they had aperitifed, wined, dined, coffeed and creme-de-menthed her far in excess of their normal intake, there was a ten-minute pause, at the end of which the girl turned to the son and said plaintively, 'I say George, d'you think your Mum's got any cocoa?'

It is a mistake to allow guests anywhere near the kitchen, unless it be for the purpose of helping with the washing-up, at which they are generally useless anyway. They have a tendency to rifle through your store cupboard and seize upon some obscure product, wave it aloft and say, 'Oh I love this. Do you think we could have it for supper tonight?', thus throwing right out of gear your carefully pre-stocked and budgeted-for three day menu plan.

Worse still, I have a friend who seizes cookery books from my kitchen shelf, skims through them till she comes to a recipe with a page and a half of ingredients and requiring utensils like double-boilers and hair sieves, and says with eager wistfulness, 'Oh, this takes me right back to the Loire Valley. We used to go to a little restaurant there where the chief made this *divinely*. I suppose you couldn't possibly . . . ? Oh no, it's a bit much to ask, isn't it?!! (with a light laugh) – 'Aren't I awful!'

Yes, she is awful and it jolly well is too much to ask, but as she is one of those people who, come hell or high water, always gets their way, I can see the outcome quite clearly. While I am nailed to the kitchen the entire afternoon, pounding, sieving, grinding, separating and whisking, she will wander round the garden, calling through the window helpful things like,

'I say, your rose bed is absolutely CHOKED with weed', or:

'Did you know your hellebore's got blackspot?'

It saves a great deal of wear and tear on the nerves to take your guests out for all meals. It also, unfortunately, creates a great deal more wear and tear on the pocket.

IT IS A WISE HOSTESS WHO TAKES A FEW ELEMENTARY PRECAUTIONS

Forewarned, forearmed; to be prepared is half the victory.

Cervantes, *Don Quixote*, Pt. II Chap. 17

When it is impossible to stave off any longer the evil moment when you are obliged to ask someone to share your bed and board (figuratively speaking), before casting the fatal die it is as well to make a few elementary precautions. For example:

1 Make ABSOLUTELY sure that they have not recently embraced some weird, newfangled religion which is going to throw your Sunday into a state of confusion by the necessity of having to drive them to:

- (a) A squalid corrugated tin hut in the next town but three to where you live.
- (b) A basement in North London at the hour when the weekend traffic is returning.
- (c) Salisbury Plain at sunrise.

2 Ascertain that their telephone habits are at least halfway civilized. When they casually ask if they can phone cousin Maud to wish her a happy birthday, be sure to check up on said cousin's whereabouts. She could be in Wagga Wagga. When they say, 'Could I just give a quick call to my stockbroker?' stand over them, drumming your fingers on the table and listening to every word (you might even pick up a tip), in order

to ensure that they do not clog up the line for three-quarters of an hour, thus preventing *you* from phoning the butcher, the baker, your son's headmaster, the Sanitary Department about the dustbins, or even *your* stockbroker. (NB It is highly recommended to place a small receptacle for possible contributions near the telephone, but not so near as to look obvious. Protest strongly if they put any coins in it, but leave them lying there. The richest man I know actually has a press-button telephone box installed in his hallway, but you really do have to be frightfully rich to get away with that kind of behaviour.)

3 Try to drum into them the necessity for bringing everything they are actually going to need during their stay, so that they will not spend their time wandering into your room saying, 'I wonder if you could possibly lend me a nail brush/pair of

eyebrow tweezers/some cotton wool/a needle and thread/battery for my shaver/safety pin/scissors/clothes brush/gadget for getting stones out of horses' hooves, etc., etc.

4 Find out if they have any particular pet to whom they are devoted, and politely but very, very firmly make it crystal clear that said pet will not be welcome. If you are forced, by exceptional circumstances (i.e. your prospective guest is an elderly relative of whom you have Expectations), to accommodate an accompanying animal, then insist that all its accoutrements will be brought with it. The alternative will be to come downstairs to find a dog slurping its Pedigree Chum out of your priceless T'chang Dynasty soup tureen, which has been handed down through countless generations, and of hearing your guest say brightly, 'I hope you don't mind my using this old pot for Muffin's dins.'

5 By a series of subtle hints, indicate very clearly that if they are bringing a floral tribute it would be infinitely preferable to make it a plant, rather than a bouquet. The advantages of this are twofold. Firstly, guests are inclined to take huff if their offerings are not instantly put on display, and it is difficult to combine heaving up their suitcases, showing them their quarters and wrestling with the problem of trying to stuff a whole lot of top-heavy gladioli into a small posy bowl – inevitably the only receptacle immediately to hand.

Secondly, a plant can always be taken to somebody else as a gift after they have gone. By the same series of subtle hints, try to make it plain that a bottle of Scotch would be better still. If you do not seem to be getting the message across, become less subtle.

6 Make it plain that their reception will be cold to the point of frost-bite if they arrive with a whole lot of impedimenta with which they intend cluttering up your house whilst they 'just pop over to France for three weeks', on the grounds that they are sure you wouldn't mind. Point out that you would.

7 Ensure from the start that the day, hour, and preferably the minute, of their departure is firmly understood before they cross your threshold. In order to avoid the slightest margin for error a train timetable, with a suitable train time underlined, should be stuck in their dressing table mirror. If they arrive by car, it should be driven round to the front of the house on the morning of their departure and left in full view of their window. The temptation to leave the engine runnning should be resisted on grounds of politeness.

8 It is a wise precaution to ascertain, before issuing any invitation, that guests have an unbreakable engagement (like tea with the Queen, or, better still, an appearance on 'Wogan'), on the day immediately following their departure date. This will make it absolutely impossible for them to suggest prolonging their stay.

TRAVELLING LIGHT

The affluence of some guests was breathtaking. It used to take three Rolls Royces to bring two talked-about sisters to one country house I knew. They never visited more than two nights, but what a retinue!

One of the sisters was rather abandoned for those days (1930s). She was able to drive and insisted on doing so.

The pair came in that year's Rolls, their head chauffeur followed in the previous year's model (in case of a puncture or other mishap). The second chauffeur, two ladies' maids with their own luggage and the ladies' jewels in the third Rolls, and to complete the convoy, the third chauffeur with luggage in a Humber shooting brake.

Eileen Balderson and Douglas Goodland,
Backstairs Life in a Country House

Guests should be discouraged from bringing an over-abundance of luggage. If given their head they will spend their time wandering into the hostess's room, saying, 'I wonder if I could just hang these in your wardrobe. Mine's full.'

By some kind of natural growth their clobber will automatically expand during their stay, and straps will be demanded to achieve some semblance of closure of their cases on their departure.

They will inevitably leave a great deal behind.

A LITTLE SOMETHING ON A TRAY

In a grand household the staff can provide breakfast in bed, but should be tipped at the end of the stay for the extra work they do.

Angela Lansbury, *Etiquette for Every Occasion*

Any hostess who has been through the mill will know that there is only one possible place for guests to be until ten o'clock in the morning, and that is in their bedroom. (If you can possibly keep them there until lunchtime, so much the better.) The only blight is the preparation of a breakfast tray, which needs more implements, receptacles, napery and drapery for even a frugal breakfast than one would believe possible. (Any tentative enquiry from a guest about cooked food in the morning should be nipped sharply in the bud before it has the faintest chance of flowering.)

However many trays one has it is one of the laws of nature that one will never have one big enough to accommodate:

A fruit plate
A cereal bowl
A toast plate
A cup and saucer
A coffee/tea pot
A tea strainer
A milk jug
A sugar bowl
A toast rack
A butter dish
A marmalade pot
A fruit knife and fork
A cereal spoon
A butter knife
A knife for spreading toast
A marmalade spoon
A tea spoon
A breakfast napkin

and a dinky little vase for putting one flower freshly picked from the garden in, which *Ladies Home Journal* would have one

believe to be an essential prerequisite for anyone wishing to be deemed worthy of the title 'hostess'.

One can either jumble everything together on a tray two sizes too small, so that the guest will be forced, whilst eating, to be continually taking cups out of sugar bowls and removing plates from under teapots and so on, and so on, or go out and buy a bigger tray, for which one will never afterwards find a resting place in the kitchen.

When the hostess is finally placing the tray on the guest's knee, she must remind herself – when the first thing the guest says is, 'I suppose you haven't got any honey by any chance, have you?' – that it is not socially acceptable to throw the whole lot in the guest's face.

NOBODY IS PERFECT

> Left alone, the Duke prowled about the room for some moments, chewing his moustache and examining his surroundings with popping eyes. He opened drawers, looked at books, stared at pictures, fiddled with pens and paper-knives. He picked up a photograph of Mr. Schoonmaker and thought how right he had been in comparing his head to a pumpkin. He read the letter Lady Constance had been writing. Then, having exhausted all the entertainment the room had to offer, he sat down at the desk and gave himself up to thoughts of Lord Emsworth and the Empress.
>
> P. G. Wodehouse, *Service With a Smile*

Exemplary guests are those who can be trusted to use their hosts' bathroom without yielding to the temptation of making a detailed examination of the entire contents of their medicine cabinet.

Exemplary guests are rare.

Super-exemplary guests are those who not only resist the lure of the medicine cabinet but who, when seated at their hosts' writing desk, actually refrain from peering into and rifling through the contents of every pigeon-hole.

Super-exemplary guests are non-existent.

GUESTONA NON GRATA

Will no one free me of this turbulent priest?

Attributed to King Henry II

Those of us who live in the equivalent of 'The Aspidistras', Laurel Avenue, Raynes Park, are usually only lumbered with stray members of our families or occasionally friends whom we 'owe'. If, however, your address is The Hall, Little Trumpington, Glos., the chances are that you are deep in house party territory and will be expected to cater for guests by the dozen. If you are preparing to receive a mixed bag, it is as well to know which type to avoid.

Amongst the category of guests it is better not to invite, men of the cloth stand biretta and cassock above the rest.

For throwing a soggy eiderdown over any festive occasion, clergymen undoubtedly take the communion wafer.

Unfair though it may be, even the most charming and hail-fellow-well-met of God-botherers causes the rest of the party to act in a totally unnatural way. People who have been counting on a long lie-in on Sunday feel compelled to bestir themselves and stagger, bleary-eyed to morning service. The shock wave crosses all barriers so that even devout atheists, though they may stick at joining the knee-bending party, fall under the spell and by some lemming-like instinct rise at dawn with the rest. It puts everyone in a bad mood for the whole of the day, even those who had intended going to church anyway (who are deprived of their feelings of pious one-upmanship) and probably also the off-duty cleric who might have been looking forward to a long lie-in himself.

As for making the party go with a swing, there is nothing

that jams the brakes on a jolly get-together more swiftly than a glimpse of a chap with his collar turned back to front. No sooner have the immortal words, 'Have you heard the one about the farmer's daughter . . . ' passed the lips of any raconteur than the sight stops him dead in his tracks and leaves him with both his jaw and his sentence hanging in mid-air.

No matter how eagerly the cleric may say, 'No, do go on. Do tell us,' the moment, and the momentum, is irredeemably lost and the party sinks lamely into a discussion on the price of Rice Krispies or the advisability of planting broad beans in autumn.

I am speaking, of course, of the normal, middle-of-the-road, stick-in-the-mud clergyman. The alternative is the new-fangled, trendy variety who will drive the entire household mad by twanging a guitar all day long.

It is a moot point as to which is the bigger blight.

GUESTONII ALMOST EQUALLY NON GRATA

To be an ideal guest, stay at home.

Edgar Watson Howe, *Countryside Sayings*

Although clergymen may win the Unacceptability Stakes at an easy canter, there are other categories of guests who are not so very far down the field as they approach the winning post. Prospective hosts should therefore be warned that it is unwise to invite:

1 Lovers. Sleeping arrangements pose a problem. Do they, or do they not, expect to share a bedroom? There is no delicate way of finding out, but luckily today's uninhibited youth will burst into peals of ribald laughter if you get it wrong. (It was easier for Edwardian hostesses, who just gave husbands and wives separate rooms as far apart as possible, and installed their mistresses and lovers nearby. The Edwardians had larger houses. Door hinges were regularly oiled. Hostesses today, if they prefer to keep their guests apart on moral grounds, are advised to do the same.)

Do they require a double bed? It's bad news for you if they do. You will have sold Great Aunt Mathilda's mahogany monstrosity, and your guests cavorting about on one of your new, single divans is going to play havoc with the springs. Jokingly suggest that they sleep on the hearth-rug, and pray they take the hint.

If only one of a pair is with you, you can count on a twenty per cent increase in your quarterly telephone account. Sod's Law dictates that absent lovers are never a few miles away. They are always in Land's End or John O'Groats, if not America.

When together, they moon around gazing into each other's eyes, and other guests are apt to stumble upon them (sometimes literally) in unexpected nooks and crannies. Conversationally they are a dead loss, their output being limited to 'oohs' and 'aahs' and passionate sighs, interspersed with intimate little jokes incomprehensible to everyone else.

2 Anyone who has just 'Seen the Light'. It does not matter what light. Whether it is Health Foods, Spiritualism, aerobics, non-smoking, you are going to be bored out of your skull before they have even crossed the hall.

3 Crossword puzzle addicts. Quite apart from sitting slumped in the most comfortable armchair murmuring conundrums like 'A bird of prey in seven letters, beginning with H' all day long, they always commit the unforgivable social sin of filling in your own favourite crossword before you can get your hands on it.

4 Gamblers. They are liable to punish your telephone bill almost as much as lovers, with constant calls to their bookmaker. If denied access to your 'phone they are always wanting to dash off to the nearest Betting Shop, and these trips usually take place just as a meal is about to be served, or when Lady Fortescue-Plumleigh-Blythe is due for tea. In the latter case they will come rollicking back to announce with relish that they have just made twenty-five quid on a dual forecast of Trumpeter and Big Boobs, and Lady F-P-B, who is President of the local branch for the banning of everything pleasurable, will instantly cancel her subscription to your own favourite charity, gather her skirts about her and leave in high and shocked dudgeon. Gamblers also frequently tend to be a bit short of ready cash and therefore have a tendency to try to touch anyone from the postman to the local vicar for a quick fiver. The postman might not mind too much, but the vicar will.

5 Two or more of the same profession. Talk of the F. T. Index, whether old Hetherington will succeed Jenkins-Smythe as Senior House Tutor, the most effective treatment for Bott's disease, or the reason poor Puffy Brownlow was Court Martialled in

Poona, will stifle all other conversation till long after the cows have not only come home, but have bedded down for the night.

6 Two or more women who belong to the same Bridge Club, Flower Arranging Society, Nouvelle Cuisine Class, etc. Same objection as above, but slightly redeemed by the possibility of hearing some juicy gossip about other members.

7 Politicians. Their habit of addressing the rest of the house party as though it were a public meeting leads to either:

A Violent arguments

or

B A state of revulsion due to over-kill, i.e. enforced cohabitation with a Tory MP will leave died-in-the-wool Conservatives feeling like sitting round a guillotine and singing 'The Red Flag', and in the reverse situation, Socialists will have difficulty in suppressing the urge to rush out and have a blue rinse, or buy a bowler hat.

Note: SDP and SLD MPs rarely occur. There aren't enough to go round.

8 Foreigners. Their disadvantages are so many and varied that they deserve a chapter to themselves.

FOREIGN BODIES

> Sympathy – for all these people, for being foreigners – lay over the gathering like a woolly blanket; and no one was enjoying it at all.
>
> Malcolm Bradbury, *Eating People is Wrong*

Guests of any kind are a nuisance about the house. Foreigners are a disaster.

The *French* will require the whole house to be hermetically sealed (for fear of *courants d'air*), refuse to drink any water unless it comes out of a proprietary bottle and expect wine (French) with every meal. They will also have a *crise* either of their liver or their nerves, discover that their temperature is the French equivalent of 98.6° and demand to be transported home immediately, long before the end of their stay. (This is one good point in their favour.)

I was once a hostess to a fifteen-year-old French girl who insisted on washing her shoulder-length hair every day, thus clogging up the bathroom, not to mention the soak-away, for three-quarters of an hour every morning. The facilities of the bath itself, however, she appeared to spurn completely, although constantly complaining about the lack of a bidet. Apparently the French prefer to top and tail themselves, without being too keen on water touching the bits in between.

Australians are likely to call for unlimited quantities of tea or iced larger at all sorts of anti-social hours. They are also very large to have about the house, and are apt to take the instructions 'make yourself at home' more literally than one would wish. Of all overseas visitors they are the ones most liable to wander with unselfconscious ease into one's bedroom or bathroom at unexpected moments. One visitor of mine would suddenly appear at any odd hour in my bedroom doorway, clad only in a bath towel and with her hair in rollers, say, 'Hey, Annie, do you have any foundation cream?', stroll over to my dressing table and pick up the most priceless pot of Parisian beauty product (which I'd been using sparingly over the last seven years) scoop out a dollop, slap it on her face, and wander out, still clutching the pot, which I never saw again. The Australians are a very friendly race.

Americans tend to go into a state of shock when faced with a bath rather than a shower. When faced with a shower they then spend more time in it than any other room in the house. Their 'cocktail hour' starts shortly after breakfast and they feel deprived if the household is not equipped with enough ice to sink the *Titanic*. Not only do they tend to want everything done in exactly the same way as it is done in America, but they are liable to become considerably aggrieved when it is not. I had one visitor who regularly, every morning, demanded why we did not have HOT buttered toast for breakfast in England, and the reply because we just DON'T failed to satisfy her at all.

Sometimes they suddenly turn turtle and call for something 'traditional' like 'English Muffins', and are quite incapable of understanding that they do not exist in this country.

Breakfast is altogether a difficult meal because they ask for eggs cooked in explicable ways, like 'sunny side up' or 'shirred', and their tendency to then eat them on the same plate, and at the same time, as their orange, puts the rest of the guests instantly off their fodder.

They also require endless glasses of iced water to take their vitamin pills with, and are subject to 'conditions' and 'allergies' about which the hosts and other guests hear a great deal. I have once prepared a handsome snack supper including such delicacies as smoked salmon, asparagus and passion fruit soufflé for one American guest, who came to the table armed with a battery of bottles which she spread around her. She was so allergic to *everything* that, in her own words, she 'preferred to take her meal in capsule form'.

The *Germans* require Black Pudding, Liverwurst and beer

for breakfast. They are frightened by our tea. German tea being the strength and colour of the urine of an anaemic gnat, ours proves to be too strong for their delicate constitutions. Their hobnailed boots make dents in the parquet flooring, and their habit of putting the verb at the end of sentences makes conversation difficult.

They are also rather shame-making to take sightseeing, due to the female's passion for wearing beige ankle socks with everything, and the male's habit of sporting short leather trousers and a shaving brush in his hat.

The *Italians* break a lot of crockery because they fling their arms about and get tremendously over-excited at the smallest *contretemps*, and even the men tend to burst into tears in moments of crisis. If their children are not with them they need to telephone Italy three times a day to make sure the bambini are not missing them, and if the bambini are with them then the hysterical decibellage of the family conversation means that no one else can hear themselves think.

Lone males fall madly in love with the next-door-neighbour, the vicar's wife or the hostess, which can make life complicated.

The *Japanese* demand an endless supply of films, and tend to say things like 'I am going out to pray on the golf course', which reduces the hosts' children to gales of impolite giggles.

The *Russians* are monosyllabic *(Niet)*.

The *Spanish* are late for everything.

The *Swiss* yodel in the bath.

LET ME ENTERTAIN YOU

Who seeks to please all men each way,
And not himself offend,
He may begin his work to-day,
But God knows where he'll end.

Samuel Rowlands, *Epigrams*

When you have one or more visitors staying with you, life goes into an eerie time warp of complete artificiality. You eat food which is quite different from your normal diet (much better), your whole family treat each other with an unaccustomed air of strained politeness (and if ever the mask slips, this is greeted as a merry jest, with a light laugh instead of the usual snarl), and you indulge in a whirlwind programme of cultural entertainment far above the customary level of your brow.

Why hosts and hostesses who would never normally dream of going within a hundred miles of Covent Garden or the National Theatre feel obliged to compel equally Philistine guests to sit through alien stuff like *Götterdämmerung* or *The Master Builder* or a seven-hour performance by a visiting troupe of Japanese actors from the Noh Theatre, remains one of the unsolved mysteries of life. Nine times out of ten both hosts and guests would be far happier nipping down to the local Granada to see 'Raiders of the Lost Ark', but somehow this is never deemed to be a suitable way of entertaining visitors, no matter how much they might enjoy it.

Whatever diversions you might dream up have to be planned well in advance of the guests' arrival in order to give them absolutely no chance of wriggling out of the assignment, or expressing a preference of their own. They are your guests, dammit, and they are jolly well going to enjoy themselves in the way that you have planned for them.

WE AIM TO PLEASE

He is very foolish who aims at pleasing all the world and his father

La Fontaine, *Fables*

If you are feeble enough to consider your guests' tastes then you are letting yourself in for an awful lot of hard work and complications.

'On Saturday we could take them to the County Dog Show.'

'But they don't like dogs.'

'Don't be silly, everyone likes dogs.'

'They don't. I remember Mona telling me that they are Cat People.'

'What an extraordinary thing. Well, can't you find a Cat Show in the neighbourhood then?'

'I'll get the local paper and see. Oh no, of course, I lent it to Doris to read that article on making Marrow Rum. I'll just give her a ring and ask her to look through it . . .

Hello Doris dear, you know I lent you the local paper . . . Oh . . . Oh I see, no of course it doesn't matter at all, I can easily run down and get another one at Watson's – well, I probably can. No, please don't apologize, it honestly doesn't matter at all. Byee. Bloody woman says she didn't realize I wanted it back and has gone and given it to the Brownies to make fire-lighters with. Be a dear and nip down to Watson's and get another copy.'

'They haven't got one. I heard Mrs Watson tell Sam Frost that they had sold out when I went to get the Investor's

Chronicle. Can't think why we've asked them if they don't like dogs.'

'Don't be silly. I know! Miss Newton at the Library is potty about cats. If there is any kind of cat activity going on anywhere she'll be bound to know about it. I'll give her a ring . . .

Oh hello Miss Newton, I am so sorry to bother you, but I know that you know ALL about cats, and I was wondering if by any chance you know if there is a Cat Show anywhere in the area next week-end? . . . Yes, I know, but unfortunately I lent it to a friend and she threw it away by mistake. Oh, would you, how KIND of you! . . . (She's gone to get her Cat Lover's Calendar) . . . Oh there is, how marvellous! And where exactly is that? Oh, as far away as that. Oh dear, if it's as complicated as that I'd better write it down. Could you just wait a second while I get a pencil . . . Damn, whose pinched all the pencils? Lend me your Parker. No I won't, don't be silly. Oh give it here . . . Right, here I am Miss Newton, fire away. Yes . . . yes . . . left at the Blue Anchor then right at the Spotted Cow. How many miles on past the church? Yes . . . yes . . . down the hill, third on the left after the last house on the right . . . yes . . . yes . . . straight through Lower Spitting and then sharp right towards Acre's Bottom and then . . . look here Miss Newton, I didn't realise it was going to be so complicated. I'd better pass you over to my husband, he's so much better at directions than I am . . . Here, you take it, for God's sake. I can't understand a word that woman is wittering on about.'

So finally, having gathered that fifty seven tortuous miles away, Slapton Parva will be holding its Annual Cats' Carnival (admission strictly by tickets in advance only) on the following Saturday, you buy four tickets and book the last available table for lunch in the most exclusive restaurant in that area, and then Bill and Mona arrive and announce that they have at *last* discovered what has been causing Mona's hay fever – it is cat's fur, and she is not allowed anywhere near a kitty any more. So, the Cats' Carnival is a non-starter, but the head waiter having been so supercilious on the 'phone, you have not got the guts to cancel the restaurant table at the last moment, and so drive fifty miles through torrential rain, and fifty miles back again for the sole purpose of eating a meal which you cannot afford and which you could have had for a quarter of the price round the corner at your local pub.

THE GENTLE ART OF CONCEALMENT

> Lady Constance was alone at the tea-table when Lord Ickenham reached it. As he approached she lowered the cucumber sandwich with which she had been about to refresh herself and contrived what might have passed for a welcoming smile. To say that she was glad to see Lord Ickenham would be overstating the case, and she had already spoken to her brother with reference to his imbecility in inviting him – with a friend – to Blandings Castle. But, as she often had to remind herself when coping with the Duke of Dunstable, she was a hostess, and a hostess must conceal her emotions.
>
> P. G. Wodehouse, *Service With a Smile*

For a hostess to conceal her emotions at all times and in all circumstances is asking too much of human nature.

It is, however, a goal to be aspired to, and in order to achieve this ideal state it is advisable for a hostess to repeat to herself the exhortation, 'A hostess must conceal her emotions' every other minute of the day. At any particularly crucial moment of social stress this may slightly reduce the risk of her yielding to the temptation of taking a swinging left upper-cut at her guest, in an attempt to knock the bones, flesh and offal out of him.

Examples of such moments are:

1 When a guest comes in from a country walk on a wet day, tramps straight through the sitting room leaving, with every step, a large clump of evil-smelling mud on her brand new oatmeal-coloured carpet, stops for a second, says, 'Oh sorry, I ought to have changed my shoes', and then carries straight on, all the way up to the bedroom.

2 When a guest appears at the kitchen door the second after she has just dropped a large dollop of scrambled egg on the floor, thus obliging her to scrape it up and put it in the rubbish bin, instead of putting it back on the dish and serving it up with the meal, as she would normally have done.

3 When a guest whom she has left sitting comfortably in the living room with a decanter and a glass at his elbow, a copy of the *Sporting Life* in one hand and the Television Remote Control switch in the other, comes weaving into the kitchen (having made more use of the decanter than accords strictly with the rules of acceptable etiquette), props himself against the door jamb and says, 'I was bored – you don't mind if I talk to you

whilst you cook', at the moment when she is trying to remember whether or not she had already salted the boeuf bourgignon, thus ruining, in one fell swoop, her concentration, her temper and the meal.

4 When a guest, with an expansive gesture, sends crashing to the floor in a thousand pieces the priceless Ming vase which the hostess not only appreciates for its beauty and has relied on to stand her in good stead if ever her husband should abandon her for a bimbo. A Punch cartoon by Anton once nicely illustrated this situation with a grimly smiling hostess saying, 'Oh, please think nothing of it. I am always doing irreparable damage to irreplaceable objects in other people's houses'.

5 When, after having leapt into a stone-cold bath, a hostess encounters a grinning guest who says blithely, 'Oh, by the way, I forgot to ask you whether there was enough hot water in the tank for me to take a bath at tea-time!'

6 When a guest says, 'I hope it was all right for me to use this bit of old rag to clean my sparking plugs with' and holds up an oil-sodden square of silk which was the last remaining piece of material of an unrepeatable pattern, from which her curtains had been made, and which she had been preserving to make a matching cushion.

7 When a guest wanders in from the garden carrying the unique bloom which the hostess has been cossetting and nurturing through the whole year to exhibit at the local Horticultural Show, and says, 'Isn't this sweet? I thought I'd put it in that little vase by my bed.'

8 When a guest comes strolling into the kitchen just as the hostess is putting the last dish away in the cupboard after having washed up for what seems like a couple of light years, and says 'Can I help?'

9 When a guest actually does 'help' with the washing up by perpetually waving plates and glasses about to the accompaniment of 'Where does this go?'

10 When a guest says blithely 'Don't you worry, I'll lay the table' and the hostess takes the offer literally. She later comes into the dining room just before the meal to find the guest immersed in *Cosmopolitan* at the naked dining table whereupon the guest says 'Sorry, I was just going to do that' and watches as the hostess lays it herself.

11 When a guest ostentatiously asks the hostess to order *The Times* for them, and then swoops on her *Daily Mail*, hogs it throughout the morning, and leaves it with all the pages turned inside out and not folded in the correct creases.

12 When a guest catches the hostess helping herself to a large, morale-boosting Scotch from the drinks cupboard before the polite evening session with the guests begins.

13 When a guest walks in on the hostess just as she is in the act of decanting a wholesale, jumbo-sized bottle of Cyprus sherry into a Dry Sack bottle kept specially for the purpose.

14 When a guest states firmly that he/she does not like having breakfast in bed and resolutely refuses to bc bludgeoned by the hostess into accepting some. (On mature reflection it is too much to expect a hostess to conceal her emotions in these last circumstances. Better to verify the fact before issuing the invitation – and then not issue it.)

SILENCE IS GOLDEN

> My evening visitors, if they cannot see the clock, should find the time in my face.
>
> Ralph Waldo Emerson, *Journals*

The role of an hostess is such a demanding and exhausting one that towards the evening she inevitably begins to flag. She has spent her day entertaining, feeding, transporting and generally ministering to her guest(s) and after the evening meal all she wants to do is to put her feet up and drop off in front of the television set.

Not so the guests, who have spent *their* day being entertained, fed, transported, and generally ministered to and are therefore still bright-eyed and bushy-tailed.

So when the shades of night are falling nowhere near fast enough and a guest has launched into a diatribe on the lesser-spotted lepidoptera, there comes the moment when the hosts must put into practice the Art of the Long Pause.

The Art of the Long Pause is not to fill it.

The whole family must be briefed that when the guest finally runs out of steam they must remain totally and immovably silent. Even the smallest cough is enough to launch the guest back into his discourse, and all prospects of bed recede a further couple of hours. If a pause remains long enough, however, the silence finally weighs so heavy that even the thickest-skinned guests are usually moved to throw in the towel.

If they do not, once the pause has reached Olympic proportions it is possible for a host to say 'Good gracious, just look at the time. (What you were saying was *so* fascinating . . .) I must go and let Fido out.' (If the family does not possess a dog it is quite possible to give a few barks once the other side of the living room door.) On NO account say, 'Sorry to interrupt you.' The guest will immediately counter with, 'Well, where was I? Oh yes, I know . . . ' and then will go back and recover several paragraphs all over again, before starting on a new theme.

The Art of the Long Pause is an indispensable weapon in the armoury of every prospective host and hostess and if it does not come naturally to them it is well worth a few practice sessions before the guests' arrival. If necessary, take a course in Zen Buddhism.

WHEN PARTING IS NOT SO MUCH SWEET SORROW AS AN OVERWHELMING RELIEF

Now fitted the halter, now traversed the cart;
And often took leave: but was loth to depart.

'The Thief and the Cordelier', Matthew Prior

Before I learned the invaluable lesson of setting a strict time limit to a guest's visit, and if possible getting the date and time of his or her departure in writing (preferably signed by two independent witnesses), there would be moments towards what I was devoutly hoping was the end of the stay, when I would be tempted to quote from Thomas Hood's poem, 'Aestivation' that splendid line: 'Depart, – be off, – excede, – evade, – erump!'

I am not altogether clear what 'erump' actually means, but the sound of it expresses my feelings perfectly.

Lingering guests usually have thickish skins. If they did not they would not be lingering. Methods used for dislodging them therefore need not be too subtle. The following all have a proven track record of success.

1 Announce that you have suddenly been called to minister to a sick friend in the Outer Hebrides the following day, and brush aside any rubbish about them staying on to shut up the house for you. If necessary, go to the Outer Hebrides.

2 Announce that all the children are being sent home from boarding school because there has been a sudden outbreak of Legionnaire's Disease, which the school doctor has diagnosed as highly contagious. (This can be a little unconvincing if, like me, you are childless and live alone, but the names of sundry

nephews and nieces can sometimes be bandied about to advantage.)

3 Strip all the clothes off the bed and leave them lying in an ostentatious heap on the landing. If the guest makes any comment say, 'Oh, I'm frightfully sorry. I thought you were leaving today'. ON NO ACCOUNT make any attempt to supply more sheets.

4 Ask the most boring person you know round for the day, announce that unfortunately you have to be on duty all day at the Citizens Advice Bureau, and in the evening say regretfully that due to an emergency you have got to be on duty tomorrow also but that you have asked dear old Jack round to keep them company again.

5 Surreptitiously remove the light bulb from their room, and substitute a dud one. When the guest discovers the lack of light, apologise profusely at not having any spare bulbs, and proffer instead a small bicycle lamp whose battery is on the point of running out. If the guest should timidly suggest the possibility of swapping a bulb from an area not much in use, make 'Oh how silly of me not to have thought of that' noises, and manage to drop the bulb as you remove it.

6 Equip yourself with plenty of thermal underwear, then turn off the central heating.

7 If your guests are of the indoor, bookish variety, announce that the entertainment planned for them the following day is to be a cross-country charity run in aid of Save the Whales. Point out that unfortunately the BBC weather man has forecast torrential rain for the morrow, but never mind, it's all in a good cause.

8 If your guests are extrovert, unlettered fresh air fiends, announce with joy that you have managed to secure the presence of Professor Goodbody to give his famous talk on 'The Implications of the Hidden References to Greek and Roman Mythological Roots to be Found in Selected Passages from some

of the Lesser Known Shakespearean Sonnets', to the local Literary Society, and this rare treat will take place in your sitting room, from 10.30 next morning, and continue with discussions over tea and biscuits throughout the rest of the day.

9 If all else fails, serve up the breakfast butter with dogs' hairs in it.

EASY COME, BUT NO SO EASY GOT RID OF

> Withdraw thy foot from thy neighbours house, lest he be weary of thee, and so hate thee.
>
> *Proverbs*, 25, v. 17.

Despite your nightmares the sun *will* eventually rise on the glorious morning when your guest is due to depart. It will coincide with the morning on which they receive a letter from their old school friend, whom they are due to burden with their presence after you have got shot of them, saying that she is frightfully sorry but the radiator in her spare bedroom has burst and she can't get the plumber till the following Tuesday, so could they possibly delay their arrival for a day or two?

Your guest will read this missive aloud to you at the breakfast table and then will gaze hopefully at you with the eyes of a wounded spaniel. If you value your sanity you will remain stonily silent. If the silence goes on too long you will break into an ecstatic eulogy on the charms of the adorable old country pub in Winklebury (or wherever the guest's old school chum lives), and how lucky they are to have it so handy. Whether such a pub exists or not is immaterial. You will be over the hills and far away when they find out.

Having got this little contretemps under control you should briskly ask them what time train they intend catching, apologetically adding that anything later than ten o'clock will be a bit difficult for you as you have an appointment with the dentist at ten thirty, after which your day is frightfully full up. Do not specify with what. They will not have the guts to ask.

Having firmly pushed them into taking the ten o'clock train, you ask if you can give them a hand bringing down their bags.

These will not be ready. Say there is no hurry then stand at the door of the bedroom gazing at your watch and tapping your foot. Their cases, which were fastened perfectly adequately when they arrived, will be bulging out all over and they will start demanding straps (which you will not have) or plastic carrier bags or the loan of one of your cases. (Stick firmly to plastic bags.) It is a good idea at this moment to make a quick check on your towels and other linen.

Whilst you are driving them to the station they will suddenly remember that they never went back to collect that book they ordered and wonder if it would be possible to make a detour by way of W. H. Smith? No, it would not, if they are going to catch the ten o'clock train. A desperate decision confronts you. You have to weigh up the relative nuisance value of another hour and a half of their company (till the next train) against the fag of having to parcel up their beastly book and post it on to them.

Take my advice. Never hesitate. Always, *always* opt for putting the guest on the early train. You are bound to have to send things on to them, and a guest who stays an extra hour and a half could easily have some mishap which could cause them to stay for days, or even weeks, longer. If you have not read or seen 'The Man Who Came to Dinner', do it now!

The detour abandoned, you will arrive at the railway station in plenty of time to buy the ticket but ensure that you purchase it yourself (cost at this delicate point is immaterial) and hang onto it until your guest is aboard the train. Guests have a nasty habit of mislaying tickets.

Hasty farewells are said and to your horror you hear yourself imploring your guest to 'come again soon'. The guard takes so long to blow his whistle that you think he must have died of sleeping sickness, but finally the magical moment arrives when the train begins to move away from the platform; a sight which has roughly the same effect on your heart as daffodils had on Wordsworth's. As the train gathers momentum your friend leans out of the window and screams, 'Oh, by the way, I forgot to tell you . . . ' but luckily the rest of the sentence is drowned by the screech of the whistle and with rising spirits you realise you have been saved one final, boring anecdote.

You drive home feeling ten years younger and whistling 'Happy Days are Here Again'. You open your front door and are confronted by your guest's umbrella standing triumphantly in the hall stand.

This is only the beginning. You go into the sitting room and move a cushion. Your guest's knitting is nestling in the corner of the sofa. You go into the kitchen and find their jar of bran tablets hiding behind the milk jug. You strip their bed. (You have told them to 'do nothing with it', and they have taken you at your word.) Their hot water bottle is in it. There is also an unsavoury-looking handkerchief tucked under the pillow. You open the bathroom cupboard and an electric shaver falls out.

It is not advisable to rush enthusiastically into wrapping these things into parcels. (Umbrellas are not the easiest things to parcel up anyway.) As the week wears on it will be a perpetual game of 'Hunt the Guest's Goodies' as all sorts of unlikely things turn up in unexpected places, and there is always that book from Smith's to be dealt with as well.

The sting in the tail comes when you receive a plaintive telephone call from your guest to say you've sent a bundle of clothes that doesn't belong to them. You realize that you've forwarded the bag of unwashed mending that you have been meaning to 'see to' before their arrival and had hastily hidden in a drawer in the spare room. Given the condition of the clothes, you can only reflect thankfully that it will probably put your guest off ever coming to stay again.

Unbidden guests are often welcomest when they are gone.

Shakespeare, *Henry VI*, Act II, Sc. 2.

Is the man mad? ALL guests are welcomest when they are gone!

WHEN THE BALL AND CHAIN IS ROUND THE OTHER ANKLE

PROFESSIONALS vs AMATEURS

> There's a small hotel,
> With a wishing well,
> I wish that we were there . . .'
>
> Lorenz Hart, *On Your Toes*

After all, what are hotels for? Who am I to take the bread out of the mouths of starving hoteliers? You go to their establishments; you click your fingers and you ring bells, you order the exact meals that you want, when you want them, and hang 'Do Not Disturb' signs outside your bedroom door. Try doing any of these things in other people's houses and see where it gets you.

I can never see the point of going and staying in other people's houses. Why exchange your home comforts for the discomforts of somebody else's home?

You never know where the warm corners are in other people's houses. It's trial and error to find the most comfortable chair, and when you've found it the dog will have got to it first. You have to be on your best behaviour the whole time, never complaining of draughts, or lumpy beds, or the temperature at which the food is served. You are frequently expected to 'pull your weight' with the housework (whilst the dust is mounting up, untouched, in layers, in your own home) and you are always supposed to 'join in' things, and to show an animated interest in any topic of conversation, no matter how boring. You're supposed to contribute to the gaiety of the gathering by sparkling, and being stimulating. And at the end of it all you are supposed to thank someone.

If you accidentally spill some ink, wine, nail-varnish or cough mixture on the carpet in other people's houses you have to get down on your hands and knees and scrub till the colour becomes slightly less garish, and then give yourself a hernia pushing the chest of drawers into a position which conceals the resulting stain. Till the end of your visit there will be tell-tale indentations in the carpet which scream all too clearly of the chest's normal resting place. In hotels you just ring for a minion to mop up the mess.

Similarly, if you break an item of glass or china in other people's houses you have to huddle the bits under your mackintosh and creep out when you hope no one is looking and trail all round the town trying to match it. You never do. When you finally confess, the object – even if it is only a hideous ashtray with 'A present from Scarborough' inscribed on it – will always turn out to have been a cherished memento given to your hosts by a dear friend now no longer with us. Your host will murmur something about preferring to have lost a fortune (which is a lie) and have to be kicked on the shins by your hostess, who will nevertheless manage to convey that she too is smiling bravely through her tears. In an hotel you merely inform the chamber maid and demand a replacement. If the management is brazen enough to put it on your bill, you just strike it imperiously through.

There is a splendid anonymity about hotel life which has much to recommend it. In hotels small children don't wander into your room unannounced and ask if they can get into your bed. In hotels nobody gives a damn if you push off up to your room to read a book directly after dinner. In hotels you eat your breakfast in blissful silence, at your own little table, and afterwards you can talk to people or not, as the fancy takes you, and if it does not take you, nobody gets ratty about it.

In hotels you are not expected to 'contribute' in any way. Well, except money, of course, but a quid or two seems a small price to pay for not having to be heartily bonhomous to hosts and fellow guests, and join in a whole gamut of uncongenial activities. Anyway, apart from what you pay in boredom, irritation and discomfort, you are expected to bring a bottle of cheer for your hosts, take them out to dinner a couple of times, slip their offspring 'something to buy a few sweets with', and, if there is a lady 'what does', to leave her a note-stuffed envelope under the ashtray on your dressing table. By the time you've shelled all that out you could have had a slap-up weekend at a five star hotel.

It is said that 'East, West, home's best'. Hotels come a jolly close second. Other people's houses, in my opinion, come nowhere, but sometimes noblesse obliges me to spend a few uncomfortable days in one . . .

TO GO, OR NOT TO GO?

> Hospitality is a wonderful thing. If the people really want you they'll have you even if the cook has just died in the house of small-pox.
>
> F. Scott-Fitzgerald, *Notebooks*

It is said that George Bernard Shaw, on receiving an invitation from a particularly dreary hostess which read, 'Mrs. Charles Blenkinsop, At Home, Saturday 9th September, 7.30 pm', simply scrawled across it, 'Mr. George Bernard Shaw likewise', and sent it back.

Now that sort of behaviour is all right if you happen to be George Bernard Shaw. To be insulted by somebody who has got *Pygmalion*, *Candida* and *St Joan* under his belt is almost a social accolade. To be insulated by someone whose sole contribution to the field of English literature is a signature on a credit card, and indeed, whose sole contribution to the human race is merely to be amongst it, is regarded rather differently by the average run of hostesses. We have to think of other ways of sliding out of unwanted invitations.

I say 'we' on the assumption that I am not unique in recoiling from the idea of staying in other people's houses.

Actually in my salad days, when hope sprang eternal in the human breast, I rather used to look forward to going away. Now I am in my cold cabbage days, hope no longer springs. It just occasionally gives a flaccid lurch, and then abandons the effort, because time has wrought a sea-change in my expectations. Now I contemplate each earnest plea for the pleasure of my company with an eye which can only be described as jaundiced to the point of Yellow Fever. Experience is a great teacher.

There is only one absolutely, twenty-two-carat gold reason for refusing an invitation, which was immortalized in a song by Cole Porter and describes how, after Miss Otis had shot her lover down,

> When the mob came and took her and dragged her from the jail, Madam,
> They strung her upon the old willow across the way.
> And the moment before she died,
> She lifted up her lovely head and cried, Madam,
> Miss Otis regrets she's unable to lunch today.

Admittedly it would be difficult to use this more than once.

Less dramatic excuses which can be tried with varying prospects of success are to say that:

1 It is the week your neighbours are going away and are relying on you to feed and water their pet dormouse/canary/gerbil.

2 Your cousins from Australia are coming to stay with you. If there seems the slightest risk that the cousins might be included in the invitation, intimate that they are far too shy to visit strangers. (On second thoughts, Australians not being renowned for their timid, retiring natures, it would be safer to make your cousins come from a country whose national characteristics are unknown – say Finland.) Conversely, Aussies can come in handy if the inviter is prim, proper and houseproud, in which case you contend you can only come if your clan of swagmen, complete with tucker bags and didgeridoos, can accompany you.

3 Paul Newman is coming to make a film in England and has *insisted* on your house for interior backgrounds. Film companies being notoriously unreliable, you can always say the deal fell through at the last moment. Produce photo of Paul Newman, warmly inscribed (by you) expressing his deep regrets.

4 Your god-daughter is riding in a nearby (be very careful not to state a definite place) gymkhana, and would be HEART-

BROKEN if you were not amongst those present to watch her. Later send photo of god-daughter on pony, clutching a rosette, taken against an indeterminate background. The golden rule, when concocting an alibi, or, to put it another way, telling a thumping lie, is always to leave the details vague. This lessens the odds on being caught out.

5 It is the week of the local Horticultural Show and you are expecting to win 'Best in Show' with your prize marrow. Enclose photo of marrow – any old marrow, the biggest you can buy at your greengrocer's – write 'My Monster' on the back, followed by lots and lots of jokey exclamation marks.

6 It is the week of your children's:

School play
School sports
School prize-giving
Dancing display
Swimming gala
Fancy Dress Carnival
Sponsored Fun Run for Endangered Species.

(Note: If you have no children, nieces and nephews or god-children (see Example 4) can make useful substitutes. If the invitation occurs in the holidays, replace 'School' by 'Brownies' or 'Cubs', according to sex.)

The mention of children causes me to reflect how much simpler social life would be if we lived by the savage laws of the very young who, whenever they do not wish to do something, have no hesitation in stating so, flat out, without worrying about anybody's bruised feelings. I recall having a little chum round to play when I was a child, and at the end of the morning my mother asked him if he would like to stay on for lunch.

'What have you got?' he demanded, in a business-like manner. On being told, he asked if he could 'phone his mother, and having done so came back and said, 'I'm going home. We've got a better lunch.'

Whatever excuse one offers it will, finally, be to no avail, because hostesses, as a breed, appear totally incapable of taking no for an answer, and have skins which make hippopotami's hides seem like rice paper. Whenever I'm invited to stay with someone for a night or so ('Because I'm asking Dottie and Harold, and they're dying to meet you'), I immediately reply with a polite, and apparently heart-broken refusal. (I've heard all about Dottie and Harold, and the dying is not mutual.) Whereupon the hostess, with an obtuse lack of tact, promptly offers about seventeen alternative dates, stretching into the next decade and beyond. It is really simplest to accept the date first offered. If one is going to be lumbered with Dottie and Harold, the sooner one gets it over with the better.

GONE AWAY – BUT NOT FOR LONG

The first day a man is a guest, the second a burden, the third a pest.

Laboulaye, *Abdullah*

Whenever I am finally and reluctantly press-ganged into being someone's guest, I always bear in mind my mother's sage advice. 'Never,' she used to say, 'stay with anyone longer than four days. Visitors are like fish. After four days they begin to stink.'

To be blunt, my discomfort in other people's houses is so great that I usually have the sensation of beginning to stink after about two and a half hours. What you might call, 'that stinking feeling'.

BE PREPARED

> Delicious food and wine, but no gin before 7.30 p.m. Thirty years ago Georgio (Sitwell) and Willie Walton and I used to escape Sir George and drink cocktails in the golf club. Under Osbert's reign I found Leslie and myself similarly occupied.
>
> Evelyn Waugh, writing to Ann Fleming, when staying with Osbert Sitwell

You have been backed against a wall, a pistol has been held to your head, and you have finally accepted an invitation to go to stay with someone. So it's hey-ho for the open suitcases, and what to put in it? It is here that experience counts. As a seasoned campaigner let me rush to the aid of any beginners in the field and arm them (metaphorically speaking) for the fray. It is absolutely essential to get your priorities right.

So, an inexorable rule one (and two, three, four and five, for that matter) is that, when venturing forth into the vast unknown of other people's houses, a bottle of gin should always head the list of iron rations in your Emergency Survival Kit. (If whisky or vodka happen to be your particular sauce, please substitute accordingly.)

One can never be sure how much alcohol is going to be available in other people's houses, and given the basic circumstances of your being there in the first place, it is never really going to be enough. Long weekends of excruciating tedium can just about be made tolerable if passed in an alcoholic blur.

It is perhaps wise to distribute whatever jungle juice you have brought amongst a few medicine bottles, in case your hosts are the gregarious kind that come bursting into your room at unexpected moments. The sight of a full frontal bottle of the

hard stuff on your mantelpiece would probably (rightly) be construed as a reflection on their hospitality. If, however, you do resort to this mild deception, remember to steer well clear of any guests with incipient cold symptoms. If they plead for a dose of your cough mixture, complications could ensue, and explanations would be difficult.

Having got the number one priority item safely stashed away in the suitcase, the prospective guest can then turn his attention to the next most important item on the agenda, namely sustenance. It must be something to do with the overwrought state of nervous exhaustion into which one is inevitably plunged by the stresses and strains of being a guest, which causes one to feel perpetually ravenous in other people's houses.

Even if one gets enough to eat (which is doubtful), somehow one is always seized with a desperate craving for food in the small hours.

I have occasionally tried raiding my host's fridge. This is never a good idea. Even if one manages to negotiate the landing without tripping over the cat and the staircase whose every tread emits a noise like the death throes of a stuck pig, when one reaches the fridge, the journey always turns out to have been a waste of effort.

I think hostesses do it on purpose. They arrange the food so that it is either unsuitable for pinching (jelly, for instance, is neither easy to eat nor sufficiently sustaining to be a satisfactory midnight snack) or they lay it out in such a manner that it will be patently obvious if some ravening guest has nicked anything. A nice joint of beef, off which one can hack a few slices and then retire to bed to enjoy them, if what one always hopes for, but rarely finds.

No, there is no doubt about it, if you want to survive as a guest, self-sufficiency is the name of the game. All guests should arm themselves with an ample supply of biscuits, Mars bars, peanuts, or whatever other bland food takes their fancy. Let me emphasize the need for blandness. Products such as gorgonzola or camembert cheese are not recommended, unless you want to give rise to the suspicion that you have packed a dead cat amongst your luggage.

Other elementary precautions to be taken are to remember to gather up and dispose of the crumbs from in and around your bed each morning and, at your departure, to refrain from chucking a load of empty crisp packets and biscuit wrappers in your own bedroom wastepaper basket. If by any chance one of your fellow guests has got up your nose to a greater degree than normal, a splendid form of retaliation is to dump your tell-tale rubbish in *his/her* basket.

One last piece of advice which cannot be emphasized too strongly. It is absolutely essential to make perfectly sure that the locks on your suitcase are in good working order and fasten securely. I once had the disastrous experience, when arriving for a visit, of having my suitcase accidentally fly open in the hall, and two packets of contraband chocolate digestives rolled slowly and inexorably across the parquet, and finally came to rest at the feet of my frozen-faced host and hostess. I am still trying to expunge the next few moments from my memory.

WHAT THE WELL-DRESSED GUEST WILL BE WEARING

> Return to suitcases, and decide that if bottle of witch hazel is rolled in paper it can perfectly well be placed inside bedroom slipper, and that it will make a difference if I remove bulky evening wrap from its present corner of suitcase, and bestow it in bottom of hat-box. Result of these manoeuvres not all I hope, as situation of best hat now becomes precarious, and I also suddenly discover that I have forgotten to pack photographs of Robin and Vicky, small red travelling clock and pair of black shoes that are inclined to be too tight and that I never by any chance wear.
>
> E. M. Delafield, *The Provincial Lady in America*

Once you have got all the really essential things (food and drink) in your suitcase, there comes the question of what clothes to take.

There is no point in losing any sleep over this. Far better to resign yourself to the fact that whatever clothes you decide to take will turn out to be the wrong ones. (Male guests don't really count here. One decent suit, a pair of corduroys and a pullover and they are kitted out for any occasion. For women it is much more complicated.)

In theory, if you are going to somewhere like Nether Wallop, the mandatory gear should be old jerseys, cardigans, tweed skirts and stout walking shoes, whilst if summoned to Mayfair it's the little black number and the three-row string of pearls.

Theory does not always go hand in hand with fact. Ten to one if you go slouching off to Nether Wallop looking like a refugee from the Oxfam shop, it will be the weekend when your friends have invited the Lord Lieutenant and his wife to dinner, who just happen to have the Prince and Princess of Wales staying with them.

The only vital thing to remember is to take plenty of underwear – preferably thermal. It is an unwritten and unvarying law that other people's houses are always colder than your own. You must concentrate on underwear because it is difficult to come down to dinner in mid-August clad in a shawl, over a Shetland cardigan, over a polo-necked sweater, without causing comment and perhaps giving offence. If, however, you can stash a sheepskin liberty bodice under your lightweight wool dress you might just be able to stave off hyperthermia whilst still keeping within the bounds of politeness.

Whilst it goes without saying that you are going to forget any number of things, it is wiser to try not to leave behind (as I usually do) all the belts to your dresses.

Keep it fixed in your mind that a dressing gown is amongst the most essential garments. Without it you can have some uncomfortable corridor encounters.

I once forgot both my dressing gown AND my nightdress. Several times I almost cracked the four-minute mile getting to the loo and back in my bra and panties, and I was thankful it was not a household where they brought me breakfast in bed.

Golden Rule Remember that if you are going away for one night you will need to pack just as many things as for three months.

Platinum Rule Never finish your packing the night before your departure. You will find that the next morning you have to UNpack your hairbrush, comb, make-up, hand mirror, flannel, toothbrush and toothpaste, before re-packing them again.

DELETE WHERE NECESSARY

A sudden bold and unexpected question doth many times surprise a man and lay him open.

Francis Bacon, an essay 'Of Cunning'

In an age when everybody seems mustard keen on getting their 'rights' it is time that someone spoke up for the rights of guests. I feel that they should be given not so much the right to reply as the right to attack. After all, it is their life style that hosts and hostesses are going to play merry hell with for three or four days (or, in cases of extreme torture, weeks), and in a caring society I think they should be made aware of what they might be in for, and given the possibility to escape it.

Therefore, before accepting or declining an invitation, the civilized procedure would be for an invitee to have the right to send out a detailed questionnaire covering the salient points which can make all the difference between hideous discomfort and a condition which might loosely equate with pleasure.

Every prospective guest will have their own personal list of necessary questions, but a rough guide might go something like this:

1 Arriving by car, will I be sent:

a) A map, and if so will it bear any resemblance to the route I should actually take?

b) Written directions, complete with details of sign posts, pub names and churches, and if so will any of these landmarks actually exist?

c) Will either of the above take into consideration one-way systems, roadworks or other local hazards too well-known to the hosts to be thought necessary of mention?

2 If arriving by train, will I be met? If so, will it be by:

a) A chauffeur driven Rolls? (rare).

b) A dilapidated village taxi with a deaf driver?

c) The son of the house in a farm truck smelling strongly of cow dung, with a step so high that I will split my skirt getting in.

d) My hostess who is combining the trip with her stint in the Meals on Wheels van.

e) A jovial uncle who, while waiting, decides to pop into the pub for a quick one, and completely forgets to pop out again?

3 Sleeping arrangements. State width and length of spare room bed. If anything out of the ordinary will it be:

a) A fourposter with a suffocating surround of curtains?

b) A sleeping bag on the floor? NB If the latter, do not bother filling in the rest of this form.

Will the mattress:

a) Be rock hard with lumps in it?

b) Have a large hollow in the middle?

c) Have sharp springs sticking out in unexpected and uncomfortable places?

d) Be electric, and if so, how many times has it been known to short? A list of guests that have actually been electrocuted would be of interest.

4 Other guests. Will these be:

a) Boring

b) Hearty

c) Snooty

d) Intellectual

e) Pseudo-intellectual

f) Uncouth

g) Earnest, with convictions that do not coincide with mine.

(NOTE. If *any* of these categories is ticked the invitee should stay firmly at home.)

h) Is anyone likely to be 'the life and soul of the party'? (If so the above note applies in double measure.)

5 Children.

a) How many children have you? State age, sex and disposition.
(If the household is known to the invitee the question should read, 'Will any of your children be at home, and if so, state which?)

b) Will any of your children have invited little playmates to stay? If so, please give same details as in part a) of this question.

6 Accommodation

Do you have central heating? If so will it be:

a) On

b) Off

c) Excessive

Which way does my room face?

Do the windows:

a) Open without sticking?

b) Shut without letting in draughts?

c) Rattle?
Do I have a bathroom en suite, and if not how far is the nearest, is it in or out of doors, and how many other guests am I expected to share it with?

7 Pets. Do you have pets? If so, state breed, size and degree of ferocity.
(NOTE. Over-friendly pets – generally dogs – can have almost as much nuisance value as ferocious ones. To be over-enthusiastically licked is almost as unpleasant as being bitten.)

8 Entertainments. Am I actually going to be left to do 'exactly as I like', as promised over the telephone, or am I going to be forcibly fed a whole lot of manufactured jollifications involving paper hats or keenly competitive paper and pencil games? Ditto for outdoor activities.

As prospective guests will realise, the possibilities of such a quiz are almost endless, and to fill out a fully comprehensive one would keep prospective hosts so busy that they would finally end up without sufficient time to have week-end guests anyway. Guests themselves will doubtless like to formulate the quiz to meet their own specific needs, but for general guidance some amplification of the points covered in the above example will be dealt with more fully in later chapters.

ILL-MET BY MOONLIGHT . . . AND AT VARIOUS OTHER TIMES

> On arrival at Doncaster Station we were obliged to wait in the cold. Bridget complained that it was a loathsome station. While waiting for the car we munched a slice of stale cake which I managed to buy in the station hotel.
>
> James Rees, Milne, *Prophesying Peace*

There are three Golden Rules which hosts should (but do not) observe on the arrival of guests. They should:

1 *Be there*
Not to leave a little note stuck in a dirty milk bottle saying: 'Sorry, we've been asked to drinks at the Hetheringtons. The key is under the third dustbin in the yard – (one nearest compost heap). Plenty of food in freezer. Don't wait up'.

2 *Drive straight home when they meet guests off trains*
All too often a hostess combines this chore with 'just popping into Sainsbury's', where she does a fortnight's shopping, followed by a trip into the next town 'which is not FAR out of our way', to deliver a little posy to dear old Mrs Woolacomb, who's been very poorly lately and does so love a little chat.

Her guest, having eschewed the toilet facilities provided by British Rail, will have not only a desperate desire for a wash and brush up, but a bursting bladder to boot.

3 *Provide a pause for rehabilitation*
Nothing makes a guest's teeth curl more than the cheery instructions, 'Don't bother to take off your coat! We're going

to watch the final of the Small Bore Rifle Competition at Rampsfield, then the Dean and his wife have asked us to dinner, so we thought we'd go straight on.' You have dressed for a journey, not for standing around watching chaps taking pot shots at targets, nor for dining with unknown Deans. You will either freeze or fry, and, in an exhausted condition, will be obliged to unpack your caseful of creased and crumpled clothes at midnight. This does not make a good start to a visit.

SOME VITAL DO'S AND DONT'S FOR PROSPECTIVE GUESTS GLEANED FROM MY PERSONAL STORE OF EXPERIENCE

Experience is a comb which nature gives us when we are bald.

Chinese Proverb

A Do remember to take an ample supply of Man Size tissues with you. Thc guest room will be provided with a small, square box which disgorges twee little bits of pale pink paper the size of a cloakroom ticket.

B Don't forget to take a present for your hostess.

C Do remember not to take her the one she brought for you when she came to stay at your house.

D Do offer to help with the washing up. You should be quite safe. Any reasonable hostess will make horrified noises of protestation and tell you to sit in the armchair and read the paper.

E Don't offer a second time. They might accept.

F Do remember to place a personal order at the local newsagents, so that you can still get your regular fix of *The News of the World*, and not get stuck with *The Economist* – or vice versa.

G Don't mention that you know anyone else in the district. They will either be hauled into dinner, despite your fervent protests that they are the merest passing acquaintances, and a very sticky evening will ensue, or else they will turn out to be the people who complained to the police about the smoke from your host's bonfire, or the ones whose son left the daughter of the house standing at the altar, and pushed off with the local barmaid.

H Do take a roll of your favourite lavatory paper with you. Every hostess has her pet economy and torn-up pages of glossy magazines make a very poor substitute for the real thing.

I Don't be too gushingly enthusiastic in your praise of the water-colours that your host has inexpertly painted. You stand a very high risk of being given one.

J Don't assume that your hosts necessarily actually like you. Frequently they owe some other people an invitation and you have just been asked along to make up the numbers, or to entertain someone's old maiden aunt.

K Don't, if you are female, and staying with a host who considers himself God's gift to womanhood, be manoeuvred into a situation where you and he are left downstairs after the rest of the company has retired to bed, i.e. don't fall for ploys like being asked if you like Jane Austen. If you respond with enthusiasm your hostess will yawn, stretch, and say, 'Oh, if you two are going to get going on Jane Austen, I'm off to bed.' When she has departed it will not be Jane Austen he gets going on.

L Do try and avoid being left alone too long with even the mildest mannered host. It's surprising how many of them have wives who've never really understood them.

M Don't on any account ever take sides in a dispute between your host and hostess. This leads to:

1. Sarcastic comments whenever a contentious issue arises. 'Of course *you're* sure to agree with him/her on this.'
2. The person with whom you have sided instantly rushing to the defence of his/her mate, and the two of them ganging up on you.
3. The wife (if you are a female guest) instantly suspecting

you of having an affair with the husband if you take his side. Reverse situation applies for male guests.

N Don't go down to the local post office and send yourself a telegram demanding your immediate return home, unless you have made absolutely, *positively* certain that the village postmistress is not in any way related to your hosts' Mrs Wilkes that comes in to oblige.

THE BAND OF HOPE

Extreme hopes are born of extreme misery.

Bertrand Russell, *The Future of Mankind*

When a host or hostess begins a sentence with the ominous words, 'I hope you like . . . ' or 'I hope you don't mind . . . ', you can be one hundred per cent certain that it is the precursor of a ghastly fate, which is already firmly *accompli*, because either phrase can be roughly translated as 'Blow you Jack, this is what is in store for you, and if you don't like it, then lumping it is the order of the day.'

'I hope you like jellied eels' (or tripe or black pudding. Strangely no one ever seems to say 'I hope you like smoked salmon, or caviar, or quails' eggs').

'I hope you like croquet. We've arranged a little tournament with the Warrington-Smythes tomorrow afternoon. They're the country champions you know.'

'I hope you don't mind having your evening meal with the children at six o'clock.'

'I hope you like unusual liqueurs. We bought this one when we were on holiday in Serbo-Croatia. The local farmers make it from wortleberries fermented in goats' dung.'

'I hope you don't mind walking to the Bracewells. Jack's just finished cleaning the car, and he doesn't want to take it out in this pouring rain.'

'I hope you like dancing eightsomes.'

'I hope you don't mind missing the last episode of *Jewel in the Crown*.'

'I hope you don't mind having Belinda's parrot in your bedroom.'

'I hope you don't mind amusing the tinies while I go to my aerobic class.'

'I hope you don't mind sharing a room with Bill's Rumanian cousin. She doesn't speak any English, but she's awfully jolly.'

'I hope you don't mind helping at the Vicarage Jumble Sale.'

'I hope you like ethnic music. We've got the most wonderful collection of records and we listen to them for hours on end.'

'I hope you don't mind taking the boys to Cubs in your car. Eric's the only one who's likely to be sick.'

'I hope you don't mind catching the 7.15 in the morning, then we can drop you off when we take the pigs to market.'

WHAT'S IN A NAME?

> Before luncheon Nancy said, 'I must dash to the Beardmore. I won't be a minute, you bet.' 'The what?' Helen asked. 'Don't you know,' we said, 'that the upstairs lavatory is called after the Beardmore Glacier. It faces due North, the window is permanently proppped open so that it can't be shut, and the floor is under a drift of snow.
>
> James Rees-Milne, *Ancestral Voices*

Steel yourself to the fact that your hosts are not going to give you the best room in the house: or the second best. Their own room will face south and give out on to a vista of rolling lawns and flower beds. Yours will face north, and will look out over the dustbins, the coal bunker and the motorway.

The actual title of the room into which people welcome (I use the word loosely) their guests is a give-away in itself.

The general, run-of-the-mill middle class household will have a humble spare room. People who've made a bit of money get grander, and call it a Guest Room. The main difference between the two is that a spare room will be furnished with all the assorted junk that over the years has been chucked out of other rooms, whilst a Guest Room will be furnished with the hosts' unwanted, unused and impractical wedding presents, supplemented by some chi-chi knick-knacks and twee floral drapes bought from advertisements in the Sunday colour supplements.

On the outside of the door of a Guest Room there will be a hand-painted, porcelain plaque saying 'Guest Room' in forget-me-nots (or sometimes, more coyly, 'For Our Friends') and bordered by bluebirds and bows of ribbons. Ten to one there will also be plaques on all the other doors bearing such legends as 'Hilary's Room', or 'The Den', or 'This Is It', to protect some sensitive spirits from the stark, lavatorial truth. Foreigners staying in such houses should have these little whimsies translated for them on arrival, in order to save them from a great deal of confusion and discomfort. Imagine the agony, of prowling round a strange house after dark in search of the loo, having taken a large dose of syrup of figs, and being confronted only by the Danish equivalent of 'This Is It'.

Sometimes, if your hosts have made it big in the world of show business or advertising, you get a Guest Suite, which at least eliminates the problem of finding the lavatory, because you get one all to yourself – usually with flowers on the interior of the basin and a mock gold handle to flush it with.

Higher up the social scale, amongst the real nobs, the spare rooms proliferate to the extent of needing to be distinguished by names, such as 'The Yellow Room', 'The Chinese Room', 'The South Room', or even 'The Queen's Room', which gently indicates the calibre of guests that they are accustomed to receive, without them having to be so ill-bred as to mention it.

These rooms will NOT have porcelain plaques on the door.

If the nobs have become impoverished and so reduced to only one spare room, they tend to give it a jokey title like 'The Dungeon', 'The Deep Freeze', 'The Bake Oven' or 'The Broom Cupboard', thus indicating to the prospective guest the precise nature of the discomfort that is in store for him.

No matter what fancy title that hosts have decided to give it, there is an unwritten law of hospitality which says that a spare room by any other name will always be just as uncomfortable.

FOOTNOTE

Sometimes you won't get a room at all. You will be expected to sleep on a 'put-you-up' in the living room. This means that the amount of sleep you get will be dictated by the whims of the host family.

However much you long, on your first evening, to say, 'Would you excuse me if I turn in early tonight? It was a longish journey', you haven't got a hope in Hell of turning in until the son and daughter of the house have got their bottoms off the adaptable sofa that you are supposed to be turning in *to*. Of course it has to be the night that BBC 2 is showing, 'That marvellous Danish film that won the Art Critics Award for Symbolism in the Moving Image in 1972', and which the whole family is dedicated to watching till the (very) bitter end. Your Danish not being great you feel it could well have won the Art Critics Award for incomprehensibility, and you gaze gloomily from the clock to the couch and try to calculate how many more yawning hours of Dansk Kultur stretch between you and sleep.

The moment the film is over the whole family, with the exception of your hostess, shoot straight off to their cozily prepared, electrically blanketed beds. Your hostess kindly lingers behind to show you how to cope with the complexities of turning the sofa back into a bed. 'So that you'll know in future' (meaning that from now on you do your own hard work), and then leaves you to make it up.

Just as she is going out of the door she turns and says, with awful archness, 'I'm afraid there's going to be a *wee* bit of a bustle in the morning, because the Parish Council is meeting in here at nine o'clock!', which, interpreted, means that if you want breakfast and a bath you're going to have to get up, get out and get your beastly bed reconstructed well before eight.

Subsequently, you find that the Parish Council meeting is only incidental to your rising hour, because the living room provides a short cut to the garage and bike shed, so that all working or schooling members of the family will have come tramping through your sleeping quarters long before the lark has even stretched in its nest.

THE LIGHT FANTASTIC

I feel and seek the light I cannot see.

Samuel Taylor Coleridge, *II Zapolya*, Act 1, Sc. 1.

No matter where one stays, be it with the richest or the poorest in the land there is one unfailing rule upon which a guest can count with the concrete certainty of Monday coming after Sunday.

The bedside lamp (if there is one) will be useless.

It will be about nine inches high, covered with a conical shade which throws down a three-inch pool of light, and it will stand on a table some six inches below the level of the bed.

There will be no method of turning it on or off anywhere near the bed. Either it will be plugged in directly underneath the chest of drawers standing alongside, and you will have to crawl about on hands and knees and probably give yourself an electric shock in the process, or it will have been connected by your host in an amateur and highly dangerous looking manner to the central light, by a series of complicated looping wires, so obliging you (once you have given up the unequal battle to read), to stagger out of bed and turn off both lights by the door, then grope your way back to the bed in the dark, playing a sort of 'Blind Guest's Obstacle Race' with the various bits of furniture placed about for you to bark your shins on.

I HOPE YOU'VE GOT EVERYTHING YOU NEED

> Take her upstairs – spare room like an ice-house, owing to open window, and fire still smoking, though less – she says room is delightful, and I leave her, begging her to ask for anything she wants – (Mem: tell Ethel she MUST answer spare room bell if it rings – Hope it won't.)
>
> E. M. Delafield, *The Diary of a Provincial Lady*

I wonder how many hostesses have ever spent a night in their own spare room, and having done so, would willingly repeat the experiment? Do not bother to answer that. The state of the rooms speak for themselves.

'This is your little den', your hostess will carol brightly as she flings the door three-quarters open. It will only open that amount because a huge, hideous Victorian whatnot, which has been given them by an aunt from whom they have Expectations, and which they therefore feel obliged to keep, has been wedged just inside the door. With difficulty you manoeuvre yourself and your suitcase inside.

'I hope you've got everything you want', your hostess goes on brightly, waving a vague arm to indicate the appalling conglomeration of junk furniture. 'If you need anything else, just shout', and you think grimly that if you took her at her word you would be hoarse within five mionutes.

'I'm afraid there are one or two of Freddie's things in the wardrobe', she says, opening the door to reveal it so stuffed with her husband's suits that it looks like the storage vault at Moss Bros. Two wire coathangers from the dry cleaners hang drunkenly in a minute space at one end. 'But there, we've left all that for you', she says, indicating them triumphantly. 'I expect there may be just one or two of the boys' things in the dressing table drawers', she goes on. (When you try to open them, this turns out to be the understatement of the century.) 'But the top drawer is quite empty and it's all yours. I'm afraid it sticks a bit, but Freddie will come and see to it for you.' Freddie ambles in later, thumps the drawer a couple of times with his fist, says, ''Fraid there's nothing much to be done about that', and ambles out again, leaving the drawer as immovable as the Rock of Gibraltar. 'Oh well', you think to yourself, philosophically, 'there would probably have been "one or two of the boys things" in it anyway.' The only spaces left for you to put your clothes are two minute shelves in the bedside table and a cupboard which houses the component parts of a Hornby train set, two jumbo-sized boxes of Lego and a mound of Dinky toys.

'Now I'll leave you to unpack in peace. Come down when you're ready', goes on your hostess, 'and don't forget to shout if you want anything', she finishes, dumping your case on the one and only rickety cane chair before she pushes off.

You can't unpack your case from the chair because the chair back prevents the lid opening, so you move it over to the bed, which means you have to empty absolutely everything out of it if you are contemplating using the bed for sleeping in.

After you have pushed enough toys aside to be able to accommodate your clothes in the cupboard, you then have to find a place to put your case. It is no good putting it back on the rickety chair because you are going to need that for sitting on. You cannot put it under the bed because a rowing machine and a set of golf clubs are already taking up all the available space.

You finally pass your stay playing a game called 'Shift the Suitcase', moving it from bed to chair to floor, where you either continually trip over it and/or block the opening of the door with it.

In hotels they provide you with a luggage stand.

Having unpacked, you take stock of your room. Last year's calendar hangs on the back of the door, and artistically is a

considerable improvement on your host's grandfather's attempts at oil painting, which hang on the walls. There is a small bookcase upon which you eagerly pounce, and which turns out to be filled with *The Boys Own Annual* from 1933 to 1947, *Fly Fishing for Beginners*, *Pond Life in East Anglia*, *My Adventures on a Donkey in Outer Mongolia* (written by your host's distant cousin), *A Hundred and One Things a Boy Can Make With Matchsticks*, *Foot and Mouth Disease: A History*, and row upon row of bound volumes of the *Stock Breeder and Cattle Rearer's Gazette*. The only one of interest is *A Hundred and One Things a Boy Can Make* . . . but you do not have enough matches.

Hopefully you turn to the bedside books provided for your delectation. A swift glance at what is on offer leads to the conviction that most households are used to entertaining a pretty rum selection of guests. Frequently (influenced no doubt by 'Desert Island Discs') the choice kicks off ostentatiously with The Bible and Shakespeare, and then descends rapidly into soft porn with the literary treasures of Harold Robbins, Jackie Collins and Judith Krantz. Sometimes a slim volume of verse will be included, but much more often a collection of lewd limericks. There will also be a couple of books of cartoons of the crudely lavatorial kind, with titles like *The Belly Button Book of Bad Taste*, or *Are You Sitting Comfortably? An Illustrated Guide to the Famous on the Loo*. If you are in a horsey household you just might be lucky enough to get a Dick Francis. If you are in a *very* horsey household you will get nothing BUT Dick Francis.

However, it doers not really matter what is put out for your enjoyment, because given the state of the bedside light you will not be able to read anything anyway.

Just as you are gloomily wrestling with the windows, which will either be stuck open or shut, the voice of your hostess will float up the stairs, asking once again if there is anything you want. It is at this point that one has to suppress a very strong urge to call back,

'Yes, I want to go home'.

MIRROR, MIRROR ON THE WALL

All mirrors are magical mirrors, and we never see our faces in them.

Logan Pearsall Smith, *Afterthoughts*

If the mirror *is* on the wall it will be distorted and spotty and hung so as to reflect either the top of your head or your naval.

More likely, though, it will stand on the dressing table, which will be wedged into the darkest corner of the room, where not the smallest shaft of day or electric light can illuminate it, thus ensuring its utter uselessness for either making up or shaving.

A MOVEABLE FEAST

> Houses where everyone is punctual for breakfast are not good to stay in; the virtues so flourish there. A little laxity in the morning is humanizing. For dinner, punctuality by all means, punctuality severely to the minute; but for breakfast let there be liberty to tarry on the way.
>
> E. V. Lucas, *Essays*

The moment of truth, as a guest, comes when you ask brightly, 'What time is breakfast?'

Now I have a theory that hosts and hostesses throughout the country all belong to some secret society which meets regularly to practise chanting in unison the society's theme song, because no matter where you stay the reply is always exactly the same.

'Oh, just whenever you like.'

'No, no, but honestly', you protest, 'do tell me.'

'Just whenever you like,' they chant back, like a Greek chorus.

'No, but please, really, what time do you usually have it?'

'Oh, any old time.'

'Well, just give an *idea* (you begin to have the weird sensation that you are playing 'Give Us a Clue' and half expect them to act out the answer in three syllables.

The scenario now divides in two. There are hostesses who ask you what you actually LIKE for breakfast (presumably with the object of getting up and preparing it for you 'whenever yhou like') and there are others who say gaily something on the lines of, 'It's Liberty Hall here. You'll find everything you want in the kitchen. Everyone gets their own breakfast. Just take whatever you want, whenever you like.'

Both are false trails.

You go to bed feeling distinctly uneasy and for the first half of the night you do not sleep a wink for fear of not waking up in time for 'whenever you like', and then, just before dawn, you fall into fitful, exhausted slumber.

It does not last long. Some inbuilt alarm clock alerts you that it might be 'any old time'. Suddenly you are awake again and stand like 'The Stage at Bay', with nostrils aquiver. You cannot hear anything. You cannot smell anything. It's a dead ringer for that, 'night before Christmas, when all through the house, not a creature was stirring, not even a mouse'. Gingerly you open your bedroom door. Not a sign of life anywhere. (Even the mouse would be welcome.) You listen for tell-tale spitting and tooth-brushing sounds outside the bathroom door. There are none. Doing an uneasy impersonation of the Troops of Mideon, you prowl and prowl around. Silence, silence everywhere, broken only by the occasional snore.

Here there can be an interregnum.

You might just possibly tiptoe downstairs, and if you do you are bound to find one of two things. Your host in a rather grubby dressing gown, with tousled hair and a lot of stubble trouble, cutting up dog's meat at the kitchen sink. He will grunt, wave a vague hand in the direction of the fridge and continue with the dog's meat. He will not be pleased to see you. Or you will find your hostess, in an equally grubby 'peignoir', unmade up and wearing a bath-cap, preparing the children's breakfast. She will not be pleased to see you either. You will tiptoe back upstairs again.

The more usual scenario, however, is to skip the ground floor recce and just creep back into bed and fall into the kind of sleep from which even John Peel's hounds, with their well-known capacity for awakening the dead, would have had difficulty in resuscitating you. About two hours later you open a sleep-clogged eye and slowly return to consciousness by a process that resembles swimming upwards through treacle.

Once fully awake you are immediately aware of sounds of hustle and bustle throughout the house, and the smell of burning toast wafting up from the kitchen. You fling yourself out of

bed, rush to the bathroom and find the whole place steamed up and every towel damp, clearly indicating that all the rest of the household have been up and away hours ago. A quick splash and then you almost slide down the bannisters in your anxiety to be amongst those present.

Your hostess is there, in the process of putting away the very last of the breakfast utensils.

'Oh,' she says, but she makes it sound like 'Yeo!' 'Yeo, theah you ah'. She does not actually add 'at last' but her whole manner clearly implies it. 'What would you like for your breakfast? We've all had ours.' There is no need for her to add that, but what she obviously regards as your sluggardly behaviour has clearly got her into a salt-in-the-wound-rubbing mood. No matter how hard you protest that you do not really want any breakfast, or if anything, only a slice of toast, she is firmly out for revenge and insists on labouring to produce porridge, eggs, bacon, sausages and all the things that make you heave at that hour of the morning, and stands watching over you in an aggrieved manner as you force it all down.

If only they'd SAID.

ONE MAN'S MEAT AND TWO VEG.

> Bad cooks – and the utter lack of reason in the kitchen – have delayed human development longest and impaired it the most.
>
> Neitzche, *Beyond Good and Evil*

Even apart from the mobile breakfast, the other meals can present considerable problems.

There are hostesses who you could describe as being 'careful on the table', or, if you were being more honest, downright stingy. I once stayed with one who meted out one and a half sausages each for breakfast, and before putting the potatoes on to boil for lunch would sing out from the kitchen, 'Will you eat one potato or two?' Firstly, I always find it extremely difficult to assess my appetite before I have even sat down to feed, and secondly by decision could very well be affected by my hostess's culinary skill. I was always tempted to call back, 'If you are going to boil them to a pulp or serve them up almost raw, then I won't have any. If you are going to make them halfway edible, then I'll have three.' If the hostess had been a real chum I might just have done that, though come to think of it I would never have made a chum of anybody who could ask such a question.

At the other end of the scale there is the hostess who cannot take no for an answer, and cannot believe anyone who says they would like a small helping.

'Oh come on,' she says, laughing heartily, 'you're a big girl.' In my case this happens, unfortunately, to be true, but it does not mean that I want someone to go on ladling food on to my plate like The Sorcerer's Apprentice, till I can hardly see over the top of the mound. If it is food that I like it takes my appetite away instantly, and if it is food that I do not like it just makes me heave.

At the age of around fourteen, I went to stay with a school friend for the very first time. I was a choosey eater anyway, and when her mother served up something that looked like my father's very old bath sponge covered in lumpy white sauce, I thought for an awful moment I might throw up on the spot. It turned out to be tripe, which I had never eaten before. (I have never eaten it since.)

Timidly I asked for a small portion, which met with the usual, 'Oh, but you're a big girl. You need feeding up', and a dollop on my plate which would have tested the capacity of a rhinoceros. Manfully I ploughed my way through the awful stuff, my mother's warning words on politeness hammering in my head. When at last I thankfully put knife and fork together my hostess asked me if I had liked it. I was too full up to speak, but politeness rearing its wretched head again. I nodded.

'Good, then you must have some more,' said she, instantly ladling two more huge, sploshy spoonfuls onto my plate.

Freud could probably make out a good case for this episode being the root cause of my almost pathological dislike of staying in other people's houses.

A household definitely to be avoided is one where the host shoots or catches things. Not only does the diet become extremely monotonous, but at every meal you are expected to praise over and over again your host's prowess, whilst he regales you with gory details of the last death throes of the creature that you are in the process of eating. You will return home with a belly full of lead shot and fish bones.

Neither would I rush to stay with people who grow their own vegetables. In summer every meal will be late so that the veg can be 'picked fresh from the garden'. When you finally sit down to eat you'll be expected to exclaim unceasingly how much nicer everything tastes 'when it is picked fresh from the garden'. Sometimes your hostess doesn't even bother to serve any meat with them, on the grounds that this might deflect your taste buds 'from the true garden flavour'. Flavour is fine, but a full stomach is nicer.

If your host grows anything delectable, like raspberries, he will pick one minute punnet and dole out about three each. The rest will be being saved for the local MP and his wife who are coming to lunch the following week.

Winter is almost worse. You'll have to plough through platefuls of the least interesting vegetables which are what are left over in the deep freeze from the summer activities, and have to be got out of the way to make room for another load in the spring. If they have deep frozen any raspberries, these will not appear. (Query: could the MP and his wife be coming to lunch again?)

If you stray very far from your own stamping ground you'll have regional delicacies rammed down your throat. In Cornwall you'll be stuffed with pasties, in Lancashire you'll drown in hot-pot, and in Scotland there will be no escaping a confrontation with a haggis 'made from Rob's Great Granny's recipe!'

Nobody every bothers to ask if you like these weird concoctions. You're there, so you'll eat what the natives eat, and if you don't make a damned good show of rolling the stuff round your mouth with ecstasy, you'll never be asked again. Which would be OK.

GENTLEMEN, ADJUST YOUR WATCHES

> That all softening, overpowering knell,
> The tocsin of the soul – the dinner bell.
>
> Lord Byron, *Don Juan*

Apart from the food itself being difficult to stomach in alien households, there is also the time at which it is served to contend with. Other peoples' internal clocks can vary violently from one's own.

There are the hosts who lead 'ordered lives' and serve up meals at intervals so regular that you think they must be working with a metronome. Unfortunately, their dots and intervals very rarely coincide with the ones you live by at home.

Then there are the Bohemian hosts who seem to eat just whenever the fancy takes them. Oh, those interminable Sundays, when you hang about with a thunderously rumbling tummy, waiting for brunch, which finally comes around half past four. As Bohemians always have to do the washing up before meals, this delays the proceedings even further. Sometimes you begin to wonder if your hosts are Muslims and are observing Ramadan.

There are also households which serve a mish-mash of tea and supper around 5.45 p.m. You long to ask whether this is going to be the last meal of the day, and if so, can you have another helping; but this is a difficult question to phrase tactfully.

It is on these occasions that your store of iron rations comes in very handy.

STAY AWAY FROM THEIR DOOR

Better be alone than in bad company.

Thomas Fuller MK, *Gnomologia*

Unless you are actually a masochist there are certain types of people whose doors you should never darken. These include:

People who have just come back from glamorous holidays in places like Sri Lanka, or Bangkok, or Pago-Pago.

There will be photographs, more photographs and yet more photographs. There will also be long, boring anecdotes about how your host beat down a trader in the durbang (or whatever the local term for 'bazaar' is) till he bought a genuine, hand-beaten solid gold bracelet for the equivalent of £3.75.

People who have just come back from holidays in Bognor or Littlehampton or Skegness.

There will be the same amount of photographs and the backgrounds will be marginally more boring. The anecdotes will concern the hostess's triumph in 'picking up an absolute snip' at the local branch of M & S, where the prices are 'HALF what they are at home!'

A household where someone is writing a book.

This entails an awful lot of creeping about and talking in hushed whispers 'so as not to disturb George', having meals at odd hours to accommodate The Muse, and having great chunks of unintelligible rubbish read aloud to you in the evenings, to which you are expected to react with ecstatic appreciation.

Musicians

Their hands are so precious and sensitive that you will be expected to bring in the coal, chop the logs, unblock the drains and cart the dustbins out to the gate. The conversation will be very, very musical which, if like me you happen to be tone deaf, can be wearing.

Surgeons

Exactly the same situation with regard to their hands applies, but their conversation turns on gall-bladders (removal of), ruptured spleen, hysterectomies and amputations. It would be enough to put you off your meals if you ever got them, but you do not, as each time you sit down to eat the Great Man gets A Call from the local hospital and everything is whisked off the table until further notice. If it ever returns it is in no fit state to be eaten anyway.

Married couples whose marriages are coming apart at the seams.

A. Whilst you're helping the hostess scrape the potatoes she'll suddenly dash and shut the kitchen door and then go on and on about how Archie gets meaner every day, and how she can't stand it any longer, and if it really gets too much for her could she possibly come and use your flat as a bolt-hole for a few days? (After firmly saying 'no' to the last bit, make no further comment. If you sympathise with her you'll get your ear bashed for a further half hour, and if you try to reason with her she will burst into tears and tell you you don't understand.)

B. On the pretext of driving you to the Post Office to buy stamps, your host will suddenly stop the car and go into a tirade about how desperately extravagant Daphne is, and how he ought really never to have married her as she has always held him back in his career. (Equally make no comment, but better still, don't get in the car.)

Those lovely people that you met on a cruise to the Greek Islands two years ago, and to whom you swore undying friendship.

They will be quite different on dry land, against their home background, which will not be at all as you had imagined it. You will have nothing in common and there is a limit to the conversastional mileage which can be got out of sentences which begin, 'Do you remember . . . ?'

If female, an old school chum.

She will gigglingly regale your husband with a fund of embarrassing reminiscences of jolly japes in the lower fourth, midnight feasts in the dorm and the crush you had on a moustachioed gym mistress.

If male, your old Rugger playing comrade.

Any number of mini-skirted skeletons will come skipping out of the cupboard, providing your wife with ammunition to be used in arguments till death do you part.

People who are having extra-marital affairs.

They wil use you as an alibi machine. You will be dragged into corners and begged that, if asked, you will confirm that you went to a Promenade Concert with them last Friday – which you didn't – and could they give your number in case John/Jane gets suspicious and rings you at your home next weekend, because that's where they've said they'll be staying.

Anyone who is passionately devoted to a hobby, sport or pastime in which you have not the slightest interest.

Details later.

Foreigners in their own countries.

They too require a chapter all to themselves.

OTHER COUNTRIES, OTHER DISCOMFORTS

> 'Frogs', he would say, 'are slightly better than Huns or Wops, but abroad is unutterably bloody and foreigners are fiends.'
>
> Nancy Mitford, *The Pursuit of Love* (Uncle Mat)

Although staying in other people's houses in one's own country is bad enough, to do it in a foreign country is like doing it in a hair shirt.

In France:

You will be expected to sit on little, spindly, gold-painted chairs designed for all the elegance and discomfort of the days of Louis XIV, to shake hands with someone every five seconds and to call your host and hostess 'Monsieur' and 'Madame' for the first twenty-six years of your acquaintance.

In Holland:

You will be served cheese for breakfast and will be expected to be ready to put your finger in the hole if there is any flaw in the plumbing system. You will also be shown a great number of tulips and made to ride a bicycle.

In Russia:

You will have to crawl about all over the room on hands and knees, searching for the hidden microphones.

In America:

There will be so many gadgets that you will not dare to throw a switch or push a button for fear of unleashing a bed from the wall, putting the internal communication system in motion so your hosts can hear you swearing, or setting all the alarm bells ringing at the County Police Headquarters. You will not only be expected to talk at breakfast, but the topic will be something earnestly highbrow like Scandinavian Poetry, or the influence of Galileo on modern architecture, and you will be expected to 'contribute'.

You will be asked how you like America before your foot has hit the airport tarmac and you will have to be continually reassuring your hosts that everything in the United States is bigger and better than anywhere else in the world.

At every social event you will be wrongly dressed. 'The Thomas Schuyler Juniors are giving a champagne reception tonight' means jeans and a Sloppy Joe and not the black cocktail dress with the diamond clips in which you have decked yourself out, whereas, if you go to Brunch at the Gold Club wearing a tweed skirt and jumper you will feel like someone's poor relation amongst the swamp of women wearing black cocktail dresses with diamond clips.

'Sandwiches' will figure very largely on your hostess's luncheon menu. (I was once given hot roast beef and gravy between two bits of bread.) The rest of the food will be frozen stiff and have rather less flavour than Florapak.

The size of the 'charcoal broiled steaks from the finest Texan herds' will turn you into an instant vegetarian.

You will stand a very high risk of having Musak in your bedroom.

In Spain:

You will have to fight a losing battle against the pangs of hunger until lunch at two-thirty, and then struggle to keep awake for dinner at ten-thirty. For entertainment you will be taken as a great treat to watch the guts of horses being gored out by bulls.

In Italy:

All the curtains, towels and bed-linen will be heavily impregnated with garlic and the sanitary arrangements will be very peculiar. As *caldo* most unfairly means 'hot', you will get third degree burns every time you try to take a cold shower.

In Norway:

There is not a lot of sun; except at midnight.

In Sweden:

You will have your final evening meal at five o'clock. It will be herrings. Your breakfast and lunch will also have been herrings.

In Greece:

The Greeks have a word for everything but unfortunately they spell it in squares and triangles. So the note your hosts leave saying 'The key is under the mat' looks like Pythagorus's theorem about the hypothenuse and is just about as comprehensible.

RULING PASSIONS

> The first thing to learn in intercourse with others is non-interference with their own peculiar ways of being happy, provided those ways do not assume to interfere by violence with ours.
>
> William James, *What Makes Life Significant?*

One of the most important things to keep in mind when accepting an invitation is the fact that you are going to be a captive audience, a sitting duck, and that you are going to be forcibly fed with whatever passion happens to rule the lives of your hosts. There is nothing you can do about it. After all, you've eaten their salt (and in some cases, very little else), so you can hardly turn round and tell them exactly where to put the entertainment they have so eagerly prepared for you.

No matter how often guests are told they can do 'exactly as they like', hosts seem to feel they are failing in their duties unless they force them into doing a whole lot of things they totally dislike. Skills to which some people have been born from the cradle are not easily acquired in one weekend.

So never, never be lured into staying with people who indulge in any active hobby of which you have no knowledge whatever. You can end up looking an utter fool, or with a broken collar bone; or both.

It's useless to try to escape on the grounds of not having the right equipment. Your hosts will always have it, doubled in Spades. Their understair cupboards will be full to overflowing with fishing rods, life-jackets, riding boots, squash rackets and, for all one knows, hang-gliding gear and deep sea diving bells. None of it will be your size, but your hosts will insist that this all adds to the fun. But whose?

THE SEA

Being in a ship is being in jail, with the chance of being drowned.

Samuel Johnson, quoted in *Boswell's Life of Samuel Johnson*

Stay away from people who mess about in boats. The seas has to be in one's blood, not, as it usually is with landlubbers, in one's mouth.

However much you you may have ruminated romantically on the flung spray and the blown spume before you set out on your visit, once you're down by the lonely sea and the sky, where a Force 8 Gale is playing Merry Hell with the flung spray and blown spume, you'll realize very quickly that the last thing you want is a tall ship and a star to steer her by.

You suggest you'll be quite happy to sit on the shore and watch your hosts being buffeted about on the briney. You won't get away with it. Before you can say 'Bollard' they will have packed you into a selection of stiff, shiny yellow garments, all reeking of Eau de Billingsgate, till finally you look for all the world as though you are a fugitive from a Fish Fingers advertisement.

Once at sea, your hosts will fly with a totally foreign language, calling ropes 'sheets', and going on about mizzens and booms and bilges. At full sail your hosts will suddenly roar something absurd like, 'Abaft the focs'l and belay the scuppers', which actually means 'Duck', but as you won't have understood this you'll get hurled into the sea.

Once dried out and on *terra* a good deal firmer, your hostess will kindly bestow on you the greatest accolade known in seafaring circles.

She will allow you to gut the herrings.

THE HORSE

> Go anywhere in England where there are natural, wholesome, contented and really nice English people; and what do you always find? That the stables are the real centre of the household.'
>
> George Bernard Shaw, *Heartbreak House* (Lady Utterwood)

Should you visit the Shires, where women are weatherbeaten and men have leather patches on their elbows, you are bound to encounter 'The Horse'. Unless you were born within the sound of clopping hooves it's better to avoid any activities involving these animals. My father used to say, 'One end bites and the other end kicks,' and in this respect I'm a chip off the old Mounting Block.

Again, your hosts will talk in an unintelligible masonic language which will leave you mystified. There is a whole dictionary devoted to 'Terms Relating to The Horse'. I once got it out of the library. Under 'Huick' it said, 'See Hoick'. So I saw 'Hoick' and *it* said, 'Huick, a hunting cheer, pronounced Hike and meaning Hark.' I decided I would not go hunting.

Luckily, even horsey people usually recognise that hunting is a bit ambitious for those who have never been astride an animal before. Nor will you be allowed on any of their better animals for fear of 'damaging their mouths'. With my weight I am far more lilkely to damage their girths, but any excuse is better than none. Nevertheless you won't get off scot free. Some ancient nag, long since abandoned by the children, will be dragged out of retirement and saddled up for your delight.

Before attempting to sit on the thing you are expected to slap it, stroke its mane and, greatest privilege of all, give it a lump

of sugar. When you have screwed your courage to the point of timidly proffering your palm, the horse, sensing that you are not at one with it, will contemptuously curl back its upper lip to reveal what looks like a gargantuan set of National Health Gnashers. Then it will throw back its head with a piercing whinny and chomp down on your hand a second after you've sent the sugar flying in your panic, so all the horse gets is your signet ring and a palmful of sweat; which does not please it. It doesn't please your hosts either. They gaze at your reproachfully, as though you'd snatched a bag of bullseyes from a tiny tot.

You are also expected to draw in great lungfuls of air redolent with rotting straw, horse sweat and manure and exclaim as though it were a Parisian perfume. If you actually prefer Chanel No. 5, you had better stay away.

If you don't possess a pair of green wellies, you had better not even start out.

THE GARDEN

When I was young, I used to sing
'A garden is a lovesome thing,
Got wot'.
(Remember I was but a tot!)
But when that I grew more mature,
And ankle deep in rich manure,
You'll find
I very quickly changed my mind.

A.E.S.

Gardening hosts come in two varieties.

The first lot, the active ones, will seize your nose the minute you arrive and push it straight on to the grindstone. 'Oh goodie,' they'll gush, 'you've got here in time to help us clear the rockery,' and there you are up to your armpits in compost before you have even unpacked your case. And there you stay, bent double, till light stops play. This is when they say, 'Now there's only the watering to do.' Guess who does it? Your hostess will have to occupy herself with the evening meal while your host has to go and put out the hymn books for Sunday service.

When you finally clamber stiffly upstairs to bed your hostess will announce, 'Tomorrow we're going to clip the hedges, roll the lawn and plant the petunias.'

Staying with passive gardeners is not so physically taxing, but is a great strain on the nerves. You will be dragged round, and round and round the garden (if you try to get out of it on the grounds of having no stout shoes, they'll produce a pair from the cupboard under the stairs), expected to admire every plant they've ever propagated. Except that they are not plants, because this kind of gardener calls them 'specimens', and they all have three Latin names.

'We've a lovely specimen of *Scrofularus, friterlary calceii*. You'll hardly *ever* see one in this climate.' The thing is hideous because this kind of gardener doesn't grow things because they look nice, they grow them because they only bloom every seven years or because their natural habitat is Antartica. Unless a plant registers ten out of ten on the difficulty scale it cuts no ice. It is your hosts' prowess you are supposed to admire, not the flowers.

Occasionally, getting fed up with feeling an ignoramus over the Latin names, you nod sagely when they mention something like, *Lobengulia Caryatid Anthrax* (of which you've never heard). They round on you instantly.

'Oh, but *this* is the Mesopotamian variety, *Lobengulia, STERANOIDAL Anthrax!*' You've never heard of that, either.

It's all very mentally exhausting, and your back tends to give way with all that standing and admiring. I wouldn't mind if I could do all this admiring from a deck-chair on the lawn, but apparently that would be considered cheating. I think the poet Gray had the right idea. 'Full many a flower,' he wrote, 'is born to blush unseen.' I wish hosts and hostesses would leave it that way.

THE GAMES PEOPLE PLAY

> After dinner Ethel played some merry tunes on the piano and Bernard responded with a rather loud song in a base voice and Ethel clapped a good deal. Then Mr. Salteena asked a few riddles as he was not musical.
>
> Daisy Ashford, *The Young Visiters*

When two or three are gathered together in a strange house, some of the darkest hours are not just before the dawn, but just after the evening meal. This is the moment when there is absolutely no escaping the company of your fellow guests. You may, through the partaking of various uncongenial pastimes, have been able to escape them during the daylight hours, but comes still evening on and you are inevitably closeted cheek by jowl with them in the sitting room (parlour, drawing room, lounge; choose your own social scale) wondering how on earth you are going to live through the hours of tedium that stretch ahead before you can decently hye yourself to your bedchamber. Ten to one the torture to which you will have been submitted in some form or other during the day will have left you tired to the point of wanting to retire to bed at around seven-thirty, or, possibly, as you would do at home, fall asleep in front of the television.

Neither of these courses of action is acceptable in other people's houses.

Thankfully, 'in-house' entertainment is a thing of the past. Nancy Cunard, writing in her diary of a house party given by American society hostess, Mabel Corey, notes, 'After we heard Mrs Corey sing 'The Rosary' (Oh God!) we were allowed to go to bed.'

Nowadays you are more likely to be expected to play cards, and it is a wise move to make your card-playing capabilities known to the hosts before so much as setting foot over the threshold. I once mistakenly got myself invited to what turned out to be a house party full of Bridge fanatics. A fish in the middle of the Sahara could not have felt further out of water than I did that weekend. I was regarded as a total pariah until I finally confessed to having once taken six lessons in the wretched game, whereupon the other guests fell upon me with glad cries and dragged me instantly to the bridge table before I had time to add that the instructor had abandoned me as a hopeless case after the second lesson, and I have only carried on till the sixth because I'd paid for the course in advance, but at the end of it I still did not know my 'pass' from my 'dummy'. Seated that night at the table, not only was I weary and ill at ease, but the first thing I did was to trump my partner's ace. (For readers who knowledge of the game is even more minimal than my own, this equates roughly to scoring an 'own goal' in the Cup Final.) Nobody spoke to me for the whole of the rest of the weekend (they could only talk in terms of 'three no trumps' and 'playing the forcing two' anyway, so I was not missing much) and the local vicar had to be hauled in to take my place at the table while I, feeling rather like Little Jack Horner, was banished to a place of shame in the corner where I sat (very happily it must be admitted) curled up with a good book.

Why, in the card world, is bridge considered such a big deal? My considerable skill at 'Racing Demon' and 'Beggar Thy Neighbour' cuts absolutely no ice at all in social circles.

Perhaps even more harrowing than card-playing hostesses are hostesses who indulge in party games. Now I am actually quite enthusiastic about party games which can sometimes save one from the terrible tedium of trying to make bright, intelligent after-dinner conversation with people with whom one has absolutely nothing in common and who, with any luck, one will never meet again. If the conversation does not fall into the bright, intelligent category, then it usually descends to the level of

discussing absent friends, who, if they could hear what was being said about them, would no longer remain friends but would certainly remain absent. While this type of conversation is generally much more amusing, one cannot escape the disquieting realisation that one will, oneself, be an absent friend the following week.

In such circumstances party games can come as a blessed relief, but – and this is the crux of the matter – only if they are the simple kind with which one is already familiar. They are seldom either.

For example, I am quite prepared to play that game where you sit and gaze at a tray full of objects and then, when the tray has been whisked away, write out a list from memory beginning, 'Button, matchstick, key, pencil, cork, coin . . . ' You do not actually have to gaze at the tray because everyone always puts those objects on it anyway, which is why you have to be careful to write 'coin', and not specify the denomination, because it will be whatever was uppermost in your host's pocket at the time of preparation. I do not mind doing this because it requires no skill, so I happen to be rather good at it.

What I do mind is when some culture-conscious hostess suddenly says brightly, 'Let's play "The Lays of Ancient

Rome''!', and all the other guests get eagerly excited and say, 'Oh yes, let's', and I am left wondering what the Hell it is all about. To my horror I discover that each person is supposed to act out a well-known personality from Roman times, and the other guests have to name the person to whom he or she was married. My choice of characters is limited because the only Roman I have ever heard of is Nero. (Well, I believe there was Caligula too, but I think he was married to his horse, which might give rise to some awkwardness.) So, in a state of acute embarrassment, I feebly go through the motions of fiddling while Rome is burning, profoundly uncomfortable in the knowledge that, when it comes to the crunch, I do not even know the name of Nero's wife. Somehow I have always associated him more with concubines than wives. However, I never have to worry on that score because the other guests drawl out the answer with the bored condescension of University dons who have been asked to solve the Tiny Tots Three Letter Crossword, and then launch into their own characters who turn out to be people like Cantankerus, the third stable slave in the household of the General Tenshunius who was married to Placentia, the youngest daughter of the Emperor Plutonium. Well known by footius!

My advice to anyone who is invited to be a guest in a household where intellectual party games may be on the agenda is to read, mark, learn and inwardly digest the whole of the horrific second act of Noel Coward's *Hay Fever*, where the family Bliss blissfully play 'In the Manner of the Word' to the total demolition of their luckless guests. Sleep on it, then decline the invitation.

ALL CREATURES GREAT AND SMALL

> May 26, Sunday. We went to Sutton after dinner to have meat-tea with Mr & Mrs James. I had no apetite, having dined too well, and the entire evening was spoiled by little Percy – their only son – who seems to me to be an utterly spoiled child.
>
> Two or three times he came up to me and deliberately kicked my shins. He hurt me so much that the tears came into my eyes. I gentely remonstrated with him, and Mrs James said: 'Please don't scold him; I do not believe in being too severe with children. You spoil their character.'
>
> George and Weedon Grossmith, *The Diary of a Nobody*

Although elsewhere I have commended the candour of children, there are moments when I find it less praiseworthy.

As when a family emerges to greet me, 'with open arms', pretending that they are pleased to see me, and the child (with no pretence at all) gives me a William Brown type glare, turns to its parents, and says loudly, 'Why's SHE here?', sometimes adding for good measure, 'I don't LIKE HER.' Short and to the point, admittedly, but hardly laying the foundation stone for a happy stay. The kid spends the rest of my visit giving me surreptitious kicks on the shins and putting grass-snakes in my bed.

These kind of children are marginally more palatable than the shy sort who, at the first glimpse of me whimper, 'Mummy, Mummy!' and run and wrap themselves up in their mother's skirt. When finally forced to emerge, they back away, sucking their thumbs. With the first kind you can at least kick back.

Family pets can also be a problem. Sometimes the problems are combined.

I well remember the time one spoiled brat sidled up to me

with cupped hands, said ‘Look’, and transferred the contents of his hands into mine. The contents turned out to be a gigantic cockroach, which caused me to let out a yell, hurl the repulsive insect to the ground and execute a frenzied tarantella upon it. Whereupon the son of the house also let out a loud yell and ran to his mother, screaming that I had murdered Benjamin. And whose side do you think the mother took?

I was made to understand that the cockroach had been her adored son’s playmate ever since he had discovered it, ‘all by himself’ (with an intelligence almost amounting to genius, she implied) under the manure heap. Since that moment it appeared to have become the pivot of the household’s most tender emotions and regarded as the nearest and dearest friend of the entire family.

I apologised with as much sincerity as I could muster. It is very, very difficult to dredge up a great deal of sincere remorse for treading on a cockroach.

Luckily, on the whole, cockroaches are unlikely pets. I say luckily because guests are always expected to be besotted by their hosts’ pets and to react with glad cries and merry laughter when slobbered over, clawed, sat upon and bitten by an assortment of alien animals. Owners are completely unable to understand that you may not appreciate these attentions, and no matter what havoc the animal wreaks it will always be rewarded with a roguish, ‘who’s a naughty boy then?’, and the sort of congratulatory pat on the head one bestows on a baby who has just lisped its first word.

In contrast, just occasionally you stay in a household where the air is continually rent with loud cries of ‘DOWN!’ or ‘DROP IT!’, or ‘HEEL, I SAID HEEL!!!’, to none of which the dog responds in any way, but it makes a very unrestful atmosphere for the humans.

I once stayed with friends who had just acquired a Great Dane. My hosts assured me it wouldn’t hurt a fly, which I thought was great news for flies but which didn’t comfort me much. They then encouraged the beast to show off his friendly disposition, at which he reared up on his hind legs, placed two massive paws on my shoulders and pushed me backwards in an ungainly heap, so that I ended up pinnioned to the ground with one front paw on my chest and the other in my mouth. My hosts thought this uproariously funny, assuring me, through gales of laughter, that he was only playing. I thought this irrelevant. The taste of the dog's foot in one's mouth is extremely unpleasant, irrespective of his motive for putting it there.

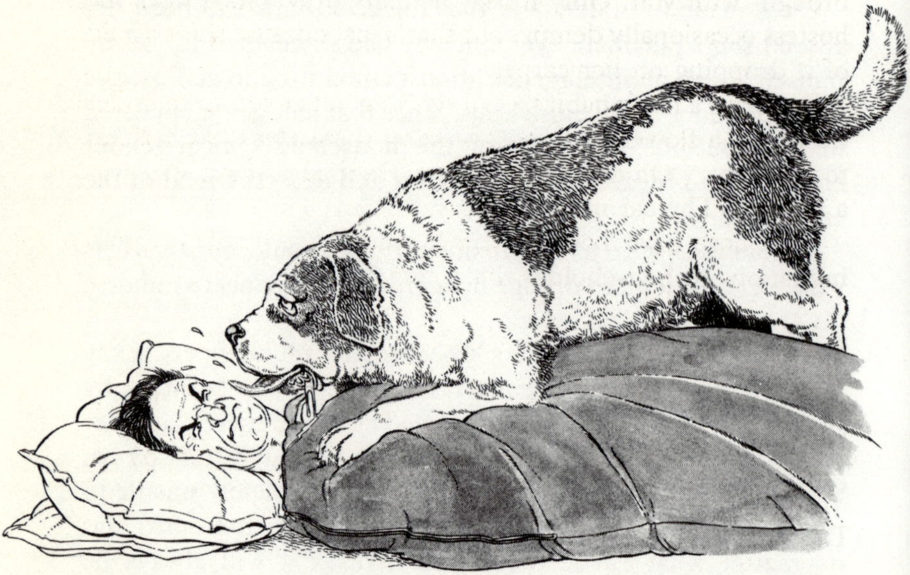

This tendency for hosts to laugh themselves silly over the suffering of their guests at the paws of their pets can sometimes go over the top. A young friend of mine, spending the night in a sleeping bag in someone's sitting room, was awoken by having his face licked all over by the family St Bernard. With his arms firmly zipped inside the bag he was powerless to escape, and every time he yelled for help he just got a mouthful of the St Bernard's tongue. When his host finally appeared all he did was stand and shake with helpless laughter.

This experience emphasizes the superiority of hotels over private houses. It's the sort of thing which very rarely happens at the Savoy.

The next most favourite pet you are liable to encounter is a cat. Cats have only to glimpse your chic little black cocktail number to take it as a signal for them to leap on to your lap and leave it covered in hairs. You are expected to regard this as an honour – 'Look, he likes you!'

You are not expected to mind it either when they savagely claw at your shins, destroying every pair of nylons you've brought with you. Only if they actually draw blood does the hostess occasionally demur, but that's just because she's afraid of it dropping on her carpet.

Cats have a nasty habit too, of dashing out at you from under bushes in a flower bed and fastening themselves like leeches to your foot. ('Oh do look at Tigger! He thought your shoe was a mouse!' The cat must be an idiot.)

Some hosts have more exotic pets, and it is advisable to refuse invitations to households which contain:

A. Snakes. You're liable to find them in the bath.

B. Mice. They escape from their cages and run up under your skirts/trouser legs.

C. Ditto dormice.

D. Ditto gerbils.

E. Ditto hamsters.

F. Monkeys. They spring round the room on the tops of bookcases and then suddenly leap down on to your shoulder or the top of your head. Once more you'll be told they're only playing. So what? It's a very nasty experience.

Take a tip from me, and if you have any choice, always plump for hosts who keep goldfish. You might be required to feed them, but they very rarely attack you. Although the mesmeric effect of watching them swim round and round may finally lull you to sleep, this is no bad thing.

GOING, GOING, GONE!

The visit paid, with ecstacy we come,
As from a seven year transportation, home.

William Cowper, *Conversations*

After what has seemed like a life sentence on Devil's Island, a light is glimpsed at the end of the tunnel. The day of your escape finally dawns.

At this moment your hosts may suddenly become pressing in their entreaties for you to stay on a little longer. Do not be deceived into believing this is because they actually like your company. It is because they are not getting on well together and your presence has provided a sort of buffer state between them. The moment the door shuts behind you they'll be at each other's throats again.

Alternatively, they will lose all interest in you the moment your departure is imminent. They will propose several trains for you to choose to leave by, and unless you choose the earliest their faces will register such horror that you will hastily revise your decision. (From your point of view it is not that you wish to linger longer than is absolutely necessary on these alien premises, merely that, on your last morning it would be pleasanter to be able to pack unhurriedly and enjoy a leisurely breakfast, instead of being hustled out to the front door step whilst the sun is still below the Equator.)

Your hostess, having completely written you off, can only think of the Hospital Book Fayre or the Brownies Bring and Buy that she is helping to organise that afternoon, and will bustle around you as a pack, asking a dozen time whether you have GOT everything. You become confused, so that no matter how often you open and shut every single cupboard door in the room, after your departure a brassiere and a scarf will manifest themselves, presumably by Immaculate Conception, at the back of one of the drawers which you have minutely inspected countless times. Your hosts will then write to tell you that they will keep these items for you 'till the next time you come', and promptly despatch them to the village Jumble Sale.

Your hostess gives no instructions about what to do with your bed linen, so, being well-brought up, you strip off all the sheets and fold them neatly, ditto pillow cases, and for my part (because the legacy of school days still lingers) I make the blankets into a 'dead man'. For the uninitiated this involves placing them in a neat roll down the centre of the bed and covering them with the bedspread. Just as you are finishing this boring and arm-aching job your hostess appears in the doorway and says airily, 'Oh, you needn't have bothered with any of that. Marilyn's coming in this afternoon to give the room a thorough clean right through,' thus implying that in your short sojourn you have managed to turn her spare room into a pestilential tip. The glance that she throws round what seems to you an impeccably tidy scene seems to indicate that she might be contemplating calling in the fumigators as well.

Your host will bustle round as well, and, if you are a female guest, gallantly and far too eagerly insist on carrying your cases downstairs and loading them into the car. It is better to be a masculine guest, whose cases he does not carry, because this obviates the inevitability of him pushing the bedroom door back to conceal the absolutely indispensable small make-up case which is sitting on the chair behind it, where it remains till after your departure.

If you are leaving by train your hosts will insist not only in driving you to the station, but on coming on to the platform with you, despite your protests that it is quite unnecessary. They are, however, determined to discomfort you by talking ceaselessly about all they have to do later in the day and how they are going to be pushed to get the last consignment of books to the hospital in time for the Fayre.

'Well, go, please do GO!' you implore, but they want their pound of flesh.

'No, no, really, it doesn't matter', they say, looking at their watches again.

When the train finally draws in, to universal relief, they suddenly break into effusive appreciation of all the gaiety that your presence has apparently added to their lives. They also spew out a torrent of visits and excursions for your 'next visit' while you mouth platitudes about how eagerly you are looking forward to these prospective treats. With luck the train will draw out before you have perjured yourself to the extent of condemning your immortal soul to Eternal Damnation.

The moment that you sink thankfully back into your corner seat is the moment that you discover the make-up case is missing.

THE BREAD AND BUTTER LETTER

There is no point in my giving advice on what to write as a 'thank you' letter. Cole Porter has written the definitive model.

Thank you so much Mrs Lowsborough-Goodby,
Thank you so much,
Thank you so much for that infinite week-end with you.
Thank you a lot, Mrs Lowborough-Goodby, thank you a lot;
And don't be surprised if you suddenly should be quietly shot
For the clinging perfume
And that damp little room,
For those cocktails so hot
And the bath that was not,
For those guests so amusing
And mentally bracing,
Who talked about racing and racing and racing;
For the ptomaine I got from your famous tinned salmon;
For the fortune I lost when you taught me back-gammon,
For those mornings I spent with your dear but deaf mother,
For those evenings I passed with that bounder your brother,
And for making me swear to myself there and then
Never to go for a week-end again.
Thank you so much Mrs Lowborough-Goodby, thank you so much.

EPILOGUE

I must make it quite clear that none of the observations recorded in this book apply IN ANY WAY to any of the households that I have stayed in latterly, in all of which I have had a thoroughly enjoyable stay, and to any of which, if I am asked, I would gladly go again.

Unless, of course, there is a decent hotel in the neighbourhood.